"No matter how groundbreaking your technical work may be, if you can't clearly convey its value, your ideas may never take off. *Luminary* is a masterclass in presentation skills for tech leaders. Jack seamlessly combines science, history, and practical templates, making it easy to immediately level up your storytelling and public speaking abilities—empowering you to overcome career plateaus."

—**Jason Jasinski,** Senior Data Scientist @ Twitch

"*Luminary* is a must-read for all technical professionals and would definitely nourish them with practical tips and tricks needed to deliver intriguing and engaging technical presentations and showcase their work effectively, thereby accelerating their success. Jack weaves together the importance of the first 27 seconds of the presentation for the speaker, the importance of storytelling style and the key pillars to deliver a successful presentation together with compelling storytelling and insightful analysis leaving a lasting impression on the reader."

—**Monika Kumar Jethasni,** Software Engineer @ Walmart and International Speaker

"I have worked with Jack on the production of the technical content for Meta's @Scale series since 2019. He and his team coach all of our speakers based on the expertise and content in his book to help with their stories (narrative, flow, messaging, etc) and the telling (delivery mechanics, stage confidence, camera presence, etc). Our engineers have a tendency to focus on technical aspects without communicating the context and stories around innovations, and it often produces less than optimal content. With the help of Jack and his team, we have been able to reverse this trend and produce content that people can actually enjoy and engage with. Luminary is a big help for big tech."

—**Francois Richard,** Engineering Director @ Meta

"Jack has a unique approach to leadership and communication. In *Luminary*, he walks us through deeply moving stories with a powerful, structured methodology to make presentations truly exceptional. This book is a brilliant guide to leading with heart and sharing your light with the world."

—**Fernando Delgado,** Cofounder of Team Techito and Ex-Google

"With today's constant distractions and cognitive overload, *Luminary* delivers a proven method to capture attention and connect with audiences—a must-read for tech professionals looking to elevate their presentations and illuminate their impact."

—**Sam Wolfe,** Senior Communications Leader, Ex-Tesla

"If you are technical and are looking to become a better public speaker, Jack has a great blend of statistics, stories, and sage advice to guide and inspire your journey. Furthermore, as you learn ways to become a better speaker, Jack thoughtfully weaves in other nuggets of wisdom, which will help better your career—which is not surprising given his years as an executive coach."

—**Matt Simonsen,** Solutions Engineer @ Grafana Labs

"In *Luminary*, Jack shares the same wisdom and practical guidance that have been pivotal in my own journey to success and growth. Each chapter is structured with clarity, building insights in a way that feels both personal and impactful. The key takeaways at the end of each section make it easy to absorb and apply his advice. This book is a game-changer for all tech leaders looking to learn how to communicate and achieve maximum potential."

—**Vish Balachandran,** Executive Director @ Comcast and Ex-Amazon

LUMINARY

Master the Art and Science of Storytelling for Technical Professionals

JACK GRIFFIN

foreword by Surupa Biswas

HOUSE ON A HILL PRESS

Copyright ©2024 by Jack Griffin
All rights reserved. No part of this book may be used or reproduced in any manner whatsoever without written permission except in the case of brief quotations embodied in critical articles or reviews.

Published by House on a Hill Press

Produced by GMK Writing and Editing, Inc.
Managing Editor: Katie Benoit
Copyedited by Amy Gordon
Proofread by Lissette Lorenz
Text design and composition by Libby Kingsbury
Cover design by Libby Kingsbury
Printed by IngramSpark

Print ISBN: 979-8-9893952-5-5
Ebook EISN: 979-8-9893952-6-2

Visit the author at www.lightupventures.com

Note: *This publication is presented solely for informational, educational, and entertainment purposes. It is not intended to provide personal, relationship, legal, financial, or other advice and should not be relied upon as such. If expert assistance is required, the services of a professional should be sought. The publisher and the author and their affiliated entities and individuals do not make any guarantees or other promises as to any results that may be obtained from using the content of this book. To the maximum extent permitted by law, the publisher and the author and their affiliated entities and individuals disclaim any and all liability in the event any information contained in this book proves to be inaccurate, incomplete, or unreliable, or results any harm or loss. You, the reader, are responsible for your own choices, actions, and results.*

Do. Or do not.

There is no try.

–Yoda

To Kallie Anna, my selfless wife

CONTENTS

Foreword by Surupa Biswas xi
Introduction: 27 Seconds 1
Act I: Empathetic Effectiveness–The Who and Why 17
Chapter One: Adapt to Audiences—Part One 19
Chapter Two: Adapt to Audiences—Part Two 33
Chapter Three: Orient Around Objectives—Part One 59
Chapter Four: Orient Around Objectives—Part Two 70

Act II: *Story*telling–The What 89
Chapter Five: Craft Content—Part One 91
Chapter Six: Craft Content—Part Two 104

Act III: Story*telling*–The How 133
Chapter Seven: Deliver Deliberately—Part One 135
Chapter Eight: Deliver Deliberately— Part Two 147

Final Act: Closing Comments–The End 171
Chapter Nine: Time Well Spent 173
Chapter Ten: One Last Story 186

Acknowledgments 191
Donations to Haiti 192
Suggested Reading 193
About the Author 194
Testimonials 195
Sources 198

Foreword

While working on my Computer Science degree, I didn't realize how critical storytelling would be for my work until I joined Microsoft. I started out working on the Just-in-time Compiler for the Common Language Runtime when the C# programming language was taking off and on C++ development tools in Visual Studio. These projects provided many opportunities to talk about my team's work. Whether debugging systems or presenting project progress to leadership, I started to notice the importance of storytelling. I observed the difference between people who presented their work effectively and those who didn't. When it came to figuring out what to say about projects (the story) and how to say it (the telling), some communicated better than others, which became a determinant to the success or failure of their technical work.

Fast forward to today, after over a decade of leading engineering teams at Meta, it has become clear to me how important storytelling is to technical innovation. Our teams continue to harness the power of the community through open-source projects like Open Compute, React, PyTorch, and Llama. Nothing is more important to our efforts than the ability to share ideas (and code!) that galvanize people across the industry to break through obstacles together and achieve the next set of advancements. However, communicating complex technical concepts is still a daunting task for many. I regularly listen to talks that share a lot of details without explaining why they matter and to whom, how one could contribute, and what can change by paying heed to the speaker. Buggy presentations cause outages and leave audiences in the dark.

This is where *Luminary* steps on the scene. As Jack shares in this book, our brains have evolved over thousands of years to gravitate toward stories that evoke intellectual connections and emotional responses, both of which are crucial to the success of technical communications. Storytelling is a mechanism for organizing information that would otherwise be perceived by our audience as random. Like all good stories, our technical content has characters—people who build with us, people who build on what we built, and people who use what was built. There are plots that surround our key characters—the challenges we faced and the solutions we used to overcome them. Without a way to tell these stories, it's hard for our ideas to catch on. This applies not just to large conference talks but also to pitching ideas in team meetings and discussing performance in one-to-ones with managers.

My passion for storytelling grew when I met and worked with Jack in 2019 to prepare a keynote talk for an @Scale conference. Over the years, I've seen him develop and ship many impactful stories, from app performance to backbone networking and other deeply technical topics across the stack. There have been a few aha moments from his work with our various teams, but one in particular stands out as a game changer. We wanted to share how Distributed Systems innovation is key to Large Language Model development and the progress of Generative AI. At first, we struggled to develop a cohesive narrative. After workshopping several ideas we crafted a compelling story around a simple yet profound message: "AI is influencing Systems, while Systems are influencing AI."

I'm excited to see Jack bring his expertise to everyone through this book. Whether you're looking to increase the perceived value of your work, rally support for it, or simply improve your public speaking skills, *Luminary* is an invaluable guide. The journey toward mastery of technical storytelling has been transformative. I hope you get as much value from it as I have.

—Surupa Biswas, VP of Engineering, Meta

INTRODUCTION

27 Seconds

In 2012, on a summer day in the Silicon Valley of sunny California, former Google executive and employee #20, Marissa Mayer, moved down the 101 Freeway to join Yahoo as CEO to attempt a historic turnaround. One of her first major moves to Google-fy the techosaurus was to implement a weekly, company-wide All Hands meeting to spark productivity and transform the culture. Following the inception of the meeting, over a thousand employees up, down, and across the organization took the stage at Yahoo's headquarters to showcase their work as part of the iconic company's transformation. If the speakers were able to engage their internal audience, they had a chance to grow support for their work and increase its impact. If they flopped—which, unfortunately, occurred a few times—their work would suffer. After working with Marissa and many others to develop and debug their stories on a weekly basis for five-plus years, I can confidently say that we not only prevented many flops but also helped many technical professionals grow their communication skills while growing the recognition of their work.

First Impressions Matter

I've witnessed on many occasions—as I'm sure you have, too—that certain speakers can keep our attention more than others, especially based on their ability to impress us from the start. This is true for every presentation, whether on a small Zoom meeting or a large conference stage.

Research about first impressions shows that we have as little as one-tenth of a second to as long as twenty-seven seconds before people form their initial perception of speakers and decide if paying attention to them is worth their time. Unfortunately, once an unfavorable impression has been made, it becomes a major challenge to overcome while trying to keep an audience engaged. If you don't believe me, recall a recent time when you presented your technical work. If it was a virtual team meeting, how many digital eyes look distracted while attendees' hands were busy typing? Or, if you were addressing an external audience at an in-person conference, how many attendees dropped their heads to their phones just a couple minutes after you began to speak?

Starting presentations strong—however large or small—is critical to avoiding disengagement. The beginning of any interpersonal experience will determine if you and your content are worth an audience's time. Later in this introduction, I'll share how to make the most impactful first impressions based on research from Harvard Business School to ensure that people will *pay attention* to your technical presentations, while you *repay* them with authentic storytelling. Authentic impressions are important because, in my experience, most engineering audiences are allergic to overly polished, hand waving speeches. If they smell phoniness at the start of a talk, they will have an adverse reaction and tune out. The goal for technical presenters is to make ingenuous impressions, not salesy solicitations.

Beyond the Beginning

Unfortunately, the potential pitfalls for presentations don't end after first impressions. Even if you start strong during a tech talk, you need to keep your audience engaged throughout if you want to showcase your work in a way that builds momentum and becomes a catalyst for you to achieve exponential success. I'll share more in later chapters about how storytelling can grow the recognition of your work, but for now, it's important to note why communicating well is also crucial for the success of your career and, therefore, your life.

I empathize with how hard it can be to articulate your technical work and its value. You may be gifted at solving complex problems with brilliant innovation but, at the same time, you struggle to curate your talking points in a way that product managers and business leaders can understand what you're saying. You do kickass work when it comes to designing architectures for highly complex data pipelines, running canary testing platforms to prevent crappy code, or pioneering industry-leading AI models but, when it comes to figuring out *what* to say about your work and *how* to say it, your efforts may be falling short. You can talk shop with fellow developers all day but when it comes to connecting with cross-functional stakeholders, you're a fish out of water ready to be filleted with questions from confused listeners.

Perhaps you aren't someone who gets stressed out by making presentations. You believe that technical professionals should be evaluated solely based on the quality of their work, not by how well they communicate it. In one sense, I agree with this. You should be recognized and rewarded for your technical prowess. It's why you were hired in the first place. Unfortunately, this isn't how it works in the real world. Research shows that tech companies consider soft skills—particularly communication competence—in their performance reviews and factor it into their decisions regarding compensation. Furthermore, a study conducted by Harvard University, the Carnegie Foundation, and Stanford Research Center found that eighty-five percent of job success comes from soft skills (such as people skills), whereas only fifteen percent stems from hard skills (such as technical capabilities). Gloria Meeks pointed to a specific individual subject in her abstract "Critical Soft Skills in the Workplace" for Walden University: "Participant P08 emphasized that a person can be an exceptional scientist, but if that individual is not able to communicate effectively with others and put his or her findings in plain and simple language, the success of that individual will be very limited. Moreover, it will be very difficult for that individual to be a good team member due to the lack of communication skills."

Technical Prowess + Communication Competence = Maximum Potential

Whether you struggle with public speaking or don't stress about it, you likely have room for improvement on your journey to becoming a luminary. I'm not going to pretend that this book is a golden ticket and contains solutions to all your problems. I can say with confidence, however, that growing your luminosity will equip you with the tools you need to shine in any context of storytelling, which has become an essential part of technical roles today—whether you are pitching a new project, highlighting progress of a long-standing effort, or simply recapping a recent project to build momentum for the next.

Why *Luminary*?

According to Merriam-Webster, the word luminary has two meanings: "a person of prominence or brilliant achievement" and "a body that gives light." When I refer to a luminary, I'm combining both definitions to make it more relevant to you and your work.

From my perspective, a luminary is someone who inspires and influences others in a particular domain. A luminary performs *dream work*, meaning she does what she loves and, therefore, it doesn't feel like work. This allows her to speak about her efforts and impact with such expertise, confidence, and passion that she inspires others to pursue the same level of luminosity. Like a Christmas candlelight service, the inspirational communication is contagious within the organization and permeates externally starting with the very first impression. From the heroic NASA Black female scientists who launched the first American astronaut into space to Elon Musk today, there will always be technical leaders who influence and inspire people as they change the world, even if you don't like how they do it. It's hard to disrupt society and please everyone.

Why Aren't You Shining?
Let's take the late Steve Jobs as another exemplary luminary. While it's admirable to aspire to Apple-like excellence, it's okay if you don't become a legend of Steve Jobsian proportions. You still have the power to cast a glowing light and share it with others. We'll learn more from Steve's storytelling strengths in later chapters, but for now, I suggest reflecting on your own journey and asking the question: *What has been holding you back from becoming a luminary?*

As I mentioned earlier, you may do incredible work, but its impact will be limited if no one is paying attention to it. If you don't earn the attention of your stakeholders with a strong first impression and maintain it with even stronger storytelling, you're at a disadvantage. Lacking luminosity is like trying to ignite interest by flicking wet matches at your audience; their attention is dampened within thirty seconds of having heard you speak. Then, if you don't explain your efforts in a way that is understandable and relatable, you will completely lose your audience and throw away any chance of gaining their support.

Endless Possibilities
Imagine an SRE (site reliability engineer)—we'll call him Relli— is

sitting at his desk in a data center (DC) managing the company's most important user traffic with top monitoring systems for perfect observability across the company's various apps. Everything is running reliably as he leans back to sip his coffee with the steady buzz of graphic processing units (GPUs) running in the background until, suddenly, *ping*! A Slack message comes in that causes sweat to drip down his back and onto his Secretlab Titan gaming chair. The message is from a data center administrator informing him that there are some people in the lobby "waiting for the tour of the DC."

"Wait," Relli murmurs to himself. "*What* tour?"

He draws a blank and then concludes that the notice about the tour was likely lost among the hundreds of unread emails in his inbox. The reality is that, when you're responsible for keeping user traffic up and running, an engineer just doesn't have enough time to read every single message.

Relli reluctantly heads toward the lobby where he greets the visitors. Since he is unprepared, he presses play on the script he's regurgitated dozens of times to various tour groups. He takes the visitors into the main warehouse of the DC that is relatively dark because they're power-intensive and Relli doesn't like to overuse the center's ultra-innovative, water-based cooling systems. He figures that the racks are stacked with the latest Nvidia machines, so the blinking lime green lights will provide plenty of visibility for the attendees to follow along. Without any introductions or small talk, Relli opens a door and leads his visitors into the dimly lit, 100,000-square foot warehouse of endless possibilities.

At this point, you might be thinking: *Cool story, Jack, but I'm a software developer and my work is different. I don't have to worry about tours and presenting to foreign visitors.*

I have no doubt that the above sentiment is true for you…at least up to a point. Perhaps you make presentations to your team. They are all fellow subject-matter experts, so they understand and appreciate all the details of your work. But what happens when you address "foreigners" from outside your team who are relatively in the dark about your content? Let's check back in with Relli and find out...

Before the last visitor enters through the doors, Relli has already made a dash to his favorite part of the DC—the region in which they deploy a super-innovative approach to rack maintenance trains (technology that regularly manages components in data centers)—where he turns on dozens of overhead lights. While the guests adjust their eyes to the visual barrage of information, Relli fires off several rounds of technical facts as he gestures at over a dozen different areas of the region in a manner like C-3PO. When he's done rambling, he shuts off the overhead lights and rushes to another area for a live demo without providing any direction on where they are heading next. He also fails to notice that a few people have hung back in the darkness to check their phones.

I empathize with Relli, as I'm sure you do, too. We've all had experiences in which people have tuned out during our talks because we failed to connect with them from the start, didn't provide natural transitions to lead our audience smoothly from one section of content to the next, or overwhelmed them with too much information. It's tough to stay out of the weeds when you enjoy gardening.

Relli goes on to surpass the record for covering the most feature explanations during a demo (31), which includes a breakdown of every architectural dimension and Pantone color scheme of the new GPU chips. Suddenly, it dawns on him that he only has two minutes of his tour left, so he races to a large screen full of real-time dashboards. It's only then he realizes that many people in his group have already started walking toward the exit. He begrudgingly tells his few loyal followers that the last stop on the tour is a live feed of user traffic sustained by the DC. The few left standing share Relli's reluctance to discuss products and users because, as they reveal, they're also SREs and primarily care about reliability. But before they have time to skim through the dashboards, the other visitors at the exit door rush back toward Relli yelling, "Finally! We know your work is important, but we're senior leaders and product managers so we struggled to follow all of your technical details. We just wanted to know how your technical work adds value to our work and ladders up to broader company efforts!"

Relli's tour could have been far more successful if he had done things a bit differently:

1. *Adapted to his audience to increase effectiveness:* When he arrived in the lobby, Relli could have taken time to ask a few simple questions about his visitors, such as their roles and interests, to increase the likelihood of achieving his goals for the tour with his audience in mind.

2. *Customized talking points based on audience insights:* The answers to his questions could have served as guideposts for the tour. Knowing his audience and their interests would have helped Relli illuminate what was important—as well as what was not—for them to see and hear.

3. *Delivered the talking points with more relatability:* If Relli had done a better job making the tour more relevant to his audience, he could have ditched the regurgitated script and spoken in a more conversational, less robotic tone for better engagement.

Relli's lesson? *Serving others serves ourselves.*

Light Them Up

It's no secret that people are increasingly consuming content digitally more than in print. Traditional paper magazines and newspapers are now largely accessed online, while social media has become a rising competitive source of news information. Although print books continue to sell, some readers prefer to read ebooks on their devices or listen to audiobooks. Digital audiobook downloads have been witnessing explosive double-digit growth for the last several years.

I'm old school and happen to love the smell and feel of the paper of printed books. That said, there is some advantage if you are enjoying the digital version of this book because you'd be experiencing a live demo of its essence and why I shared Relli's story with you. Most technical efforts—involving both software and hardware—rely on light. Whether you are working on mobile devices (i.e. platforms for audiobooks), photons on microchips (i.e. power for audiobook devices), or lines of code on a Linux machine (i.e. programming for audiobook apps), most everything you do is developed *with light* before it's deployed in *the form of light*.

Illumination is at the start and heart of most technological advancement. Light is essential for the device to be developed, to function, and to become user-friendly. Yet it doesn't end there. Development and operability are only half the battle. If you want to spark interest and ignite momentum, the light of your technical work must be shared with others. Being able to effectively communicate your ideas and illuminate others are integral parts of the process. Clear, engaging presentations pump vitality and growth into a project. If you fail to get your messages across, your work and ideas suffer one or more possible fates, including misunderstanding, indifference, or death.

Blended Brilliance

What do I mean by "The Art and Science of Storytelling" in the subtitle of this book? How will both factors help you as a technical professional?

In the chapters that follow, I offer a balanced approach by leveraging left brain logic and right brain emotion. Think of it this way:

Top rated apps run on mechanized operating systems while simultaneously delighting users with artistic UX design. Luminaries embrace and use the power of both abstract and objective tactics for the benefit of their audiences, and you can do the same.

The *art* in this book will resemble scenic stops in the form of success stories with anecdotal insights to help you identify inspirational possibilities and build your overall competence in public speaking. Art also resides in the storytelling aspects of what I am going to impart to you. The use of the word storytelling has less to do with Disney films than with the *compelling organization of your messages*. If you craft your presentation in a more engaging way by sharing relatable stories, you will intrigue your audience and therefore have an easier time explaining your technical work.

Many speakers have told me that the best advice I've given them is to break storytelling into its two primary functions: *the story* and *the telling*. By the former, I mean the content such as the narrative, messaging, key points, and slide material, so you can articulate your brilliance like Yoda. By the latter, I am addressing delivery mechanics, such as gestures, eye contact, and vocalization, so you can look and sound more like Han Solo.

The *science* part will come in the form of detailed Google Maps-like directions with pit stops along the way where you put the book down and experiment with some research-based practical tips for real-time improvement. I will ask you to try these tips on for size and reflect on the gradual growth in your skills and confidence while we resume our journey together.

To phrase it in a way that is more relevant to your day-to-day work, I'll provide you with a well-documented *runbook* for technical presentations. Like when your colleague takes a PTO day and you must be on-call to handle her system, the runbook will include flexible templates for crafting engaging content that allow you to experiment as you progress beyond the last pages of this book. For example, we'll review scientific research about how communication is received by your audience, such as the groundbreaking research from Dr. Albert Mehrabian—a renowned psychologist at UCLA (University of California Los Angeles) who discovered statistics on the relative importance of verbal and nonverbal communication.

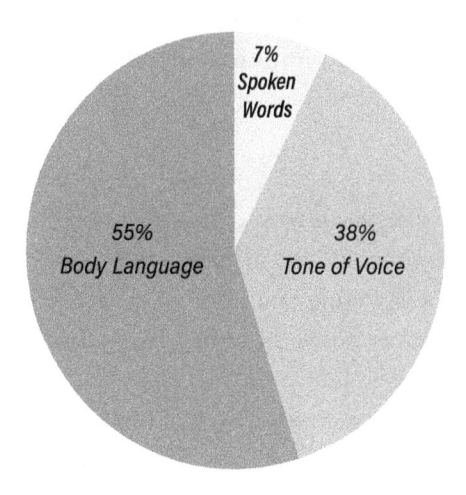

7% Spoken Words

55% Body Language

38% Tone of Voice

Why Me?

I don't like to talk about myself, but I must practice what I preach based on the research I shared earlier about the importance of first impressions. I want to help you determine for yourself if I'm worth your time.

I've worked with 2,400+ speakers for a total of 10k+ hours of coaching and training sessions with a range of professionals from highly technical individual contributors (ICs) to Fortune 50 executives. My passion for people has taken me to more than forty countries around the globe, where I have always been amazed by the transcendent power of communication.

Sharing background about my work may have earned some trust, but what matters even more are the results. Participants in our coaching and training programs experience average improvement ratings of nine percent for confidence with public speaking; twelve percent for presentation delivery skills; and fourteen percent for content development competence. While my company, Light Up Ventures—an award-winning leadership development firm—feels honored to have worked with so many top professionals on achieving their improvements, our proudest accomplishment is that we donate an average of over twenty percent of our profits to nonprofits who serve underprivileged people around the world.

My *Why*

In addition to the philanthropic efforts mentioned above, my ultimate purpose for this book is to help you navigate the intimidating arena of public speaking and guide you with story-development expertise. These happen to be the same reasons that I launched Light Up Ventures.

The spark for my company vision and this book occurred in 2016 after a treacherous bus ride from the Dominican Republic to Haiti, which led me through the darkest time of life. I'll fill you in on that experience and its aftermath in Chapter Ten, but for now, it's important for you to know that my work stems from a deep compassion for technical professionals. I sincerely admire and respect how you develop and deploy your work that impacts billions of people every day. At the same time, it pains me to witness the struggles you likely face while attempting to communicate your work. Although one of my grandfathers was an aeronautical engineer at Stanford and the other a CFO at a tech company, I'm not very technical. I have some engineering and numerical competence in the deep recesses of my genes, but my primary passion is for your plight. I have felt too much heartbreak seeing so many engineers leave audiences in the dark. I'm on a mission to help you soar and become a Jedi Master luminary with the art and science of storytelling.

Hyper Order

Before we close this introduction, I need to give you a heads-up that this book is laid out with hyper-precision and organization because I struggle with severe perfectionism, which manifests with some odd quirks. Usually, this takes the form of minor things, such as setting my auto cruise control and air conditioning only to even numbers. If you were to peek at my computer screen, you would notice right away that every object is ultra aligned: The browser windows, productivity apps, file organizer, and texting window are all positioned proportionally and evenly spaced for maximum order and efficiency.

There are some benefits of my oddities for you as the reader of the book—namely, that the ten chapters (a perfect even number, of course) are laid out with hyper order and consistency. I leverage the "rule of three" (one of the most important content principles, as you'll later discover) for the main sections—labeled as "Acts"—that systematically take you step-by-step through a scientific process, while experiencing the artistic unfolding of a narrated play. In order of sequence and importance, we'll cover the three key pillars of communication to build your overall competence:

1. Empathetic effectiveness (your *who* and *why*)

2. Crafted content (your *what*)

3. Deliberate delivery (your *how*)

It doesn't matter how brilliant your technical project is or how pretty your slides might be. If you don't adapt to your audience, define objectives with them, articulate key messages and consider nonverbals, your presentation will flop. However, if you embrace the approach and follow the flow of this book, you can grow your luminosity and blow up the Death Star of public speaking fear.

Along our journey, I will provide a few fun extras that supplement the instruction but don't distract from the logical flow. Since this is a book about becoming a storyteller, you'll read a few intriguing anecdotes—some based on historic figures and others inspired by firsthand case studies from my years of coaching and training. In addition, sprinkled throughout are occasional best practices offered as sidebars (boxed callouts) that I refer to as *sidecar* hacks to keep in line with developer language. The sidecars serve as peripheral tips to help you refine your skills as you continue your journey toward becoming a luminary.

> **SIDECAR**
>
> While we're discussing presentation navigation, let's not forget the countless elementary school devastations from when kids made paper airplanes with crooked wings and therefore never won any playground contests. Always curate and craft your content with precision to fly high with optimal flow.

On the Cuddy Edge

To close this Introduction, let's go back to where we started with the subject of first impressions. Amy Cuddy, renowned social psychologist from Harvard Business School, discovered two primary factors for establishing positive first impressions, which I attempted to demonstrate through this Introduction: *trust* and *competence* (in that order).

For *trust*, I presented explanations, language, and stories that hopefully resonated with your technical background and interests to help me earn your attention. To demonstrate my sense of empathy, I revealed my purpose and explained how I relate to your pain points. I went as far as exposing a personal struggle (severe perfectionism), which showed vulnerability and transparency. Additionally, I mentioned my company's philanthropic work, reinforcing that there is warmth and compassion behind my *why*.

After hopefully earning your trust, I demonstrated competence by sharing some background on my experience and proof of performance through my company's success ratings. I walked you through my coaching philosophy and broke down how this book is organized, so you know exactly what to expect, including sci-fi references, since I'm a proud Stars Wars nerd.

As I hope you've gathered by now, you are in good hands as you walk the path toward luminosity. So, grab your lightsaber, put on your Jedi training VR headset, and step into the virtual lobby. It's time for you to enter a brightly lit warehouse of endless possibilities as you become a luminary by mastering the art and science of storytelling.

ACT I

Empathetic Effectiveness—
The *Who* and *Why*

CHAPTER ONE

Adapt to Audiences—Part One

At 9:47 AM EST on February 20, 1962, the nation huddled around their television sets in anticipation as astronaut John Glenn buckled into the Mercury-Atlas 6 spacecraft and prepared for liftoff from Cape Canaveral military base in Florida. Americans were riveted by the concept of sending a human being into orbit and safely returning. The stakes were high, as America was locked in the Cold War with the Soviet Union, and it was imperative that they win an advantage against them in what became known as the Space Race.

The view of the massive machinery blasting into space must have been exhilarating for the millions of live television viewers. Impressive as this was, the real accomplishment was perhaps the tremendous mathematical computations that made the historic mission possible. What's more, the calculations weren't generated by electronic computers, but from flesh and blood humans—or, as they were dubbed back then, "human computers."

These behind-the-scenes heroines weren't your run-of-the-mill technical experts. In fact, they weren't even white men, which would have been the "expected norm" in that era. They happened to be four women of color—Dorothy Vaughan, Mary Jackson, Katherine Johnson, and Christine Darden—who overcame numerous obstacles and stereotypes as they applied their mathematical brilliance to the monumental effort and enabled the first American orbit around the Earth.

It is impossible to do full justice to the cultural importance of what these women accomplished. Suffice it to say, they had an enormous broad impact on the civil rights movement and, by virtue of serving as role models, helped to improve economic equality for all. If you haven't seen the film *Hidden Figures* or read the book by Margot Lee Shetterly, I highly recommend them both for a richer, more authentic understanding than I could hope to communicate. I will, however, honor them in this chapter by explaining one of the keys to their success and demonstrating how it can light your path to becoming a luminary.

Flooding

Picture yourself sitting at your desk, wrapping things up at the end of a long workday. As you log off for some digital disconnection, you anticipate having a delicious dinner with friends or family, when everyone unwinds and shares about their day. After the relaxing meal, you cozy up on the couch and settle into the cushions with your favorite beverage.

As you're about to take your first sip, you suddenly feel a vibration in your pocket. You reach for your phone and see an urgent Slack message from your manager. He informs you that he has an emergency and will be out the following day. This means, at 10:00 AM the next morning, you must take his place at the All Hands meeting and present the status update about your team's soon-to-launch AI modeling tool in front of the entire organization.

Your plan for a peaceful evening has come to a screeching halt before it's even begun. You can't think of anything except for the eyes of your colleagues upon you as you speak to them. Chills shoot up and down your spine and your heartbeat races as a flood of anxiety washes over you. You feel as if you are about to parachute out of an airplane for the first time.

Trust me on this: Nearly everyone has a fear of public speaking to some degree. For you, it's hopefully just the cliché "butterflies in the stomach," but it could also take the form of paralyzing panic. This terror triggers the central nervous system to flood the body with the hormone epinephrine (aka adrenaline), which increases breath rate, heart rate, and blood pressure; makes the hands and feet cool and clammy; heightens the senses; dulls certain kinds of pain; and causes many other involuntary reactions. These shifts in body chemistry are designed to help us make the life-or-death decision: Do we stay and do battle or run for our lives?

You've probably gathered by now that I'm referring to the body's "fight-or-flight" response, which many believe grew out of primitive instinct to protect ourselves against danger. This could mean reacting to a threat such as a charging predator, an invading enemy, or possibly from having to stand in front of the entire tribe, including the hyper-critical chief, to present the latest technological advancements in spearheads.

The average resting heart rate for women is 82 beats per minute and 72 for men. If a resting heart rate increases by 10 beats per minute because of a perceived threat, the individual experiences what scientists refer to as "flooding" caused by the fight-or-flight response. While human beings still face plenty of physical threats, most of our daily fight-or-flight responses today are attributable to stress and anxiety.

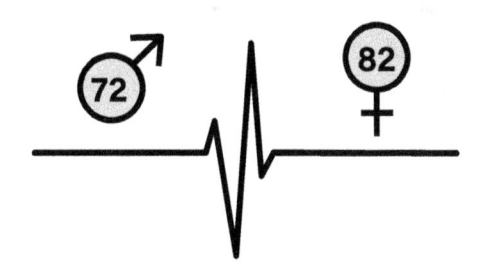

In fact, it's estimated that eighty-three percent of our stress is related to work. As if that's not enough, seventy-seven percent of people fear public speaking. Assuming you have some degree of anxiety with your technical presentations, you have two options to deal with it: 1) contact an AI startup that's developing robots and program one to present for you; or 2) face your fears.

In one sense, you can rest easy, as you are far from alone: Fear of public speaking is natural and common. You may even have heard the old joke, "People would rather be in the casket than deliver the eulogy."

I share these insights because it's helpful to understand our fears if we hope to conquer them. My goal is to offer some practical tips to help relieve your anxiety and boost your confidence about public speaking. Strategically, we don't want to numb nervousness, we want to leverage the animating energy of adrenaline for a more engaging delivery. I'll share more best practices to harness the power of non-verbal communication in Act III, but for now, it's helpful to reframe our view of nerves. We can't avoid the natural chemical response that occurs in our body, but we can contain our anxious energy and channel it for good, so it doesn't manifest as awkward physical indicators of our nervousness (*um, like, ugh, sorta*). Our goal is *to appear* more confident on the outside, even when we feel nervous on the inside.

When it comes to reducing anxiety about presentations, we need to be methodical in our preparation to avoid a premature takeoff.

Prepared to Launch

A recent study found that seventy percent of business mistakes are rooted in poor communication. Despite these stats, only twenty-five percent of leaders spend more than two hours preparing for high-stakes presentations. My point? Prioritizing and investing the right amount of time for prudent preparation ensures you will have the brightest outcomes.

You might be thinking, *Okay, Jack, I get it—but I'm totally swamped. How do I carve out more time for presentation preparation? I don't even know where to start.*

I'll share my secret with you. It's all about *understanding the variables*. To explain what I mean by this, please bear with me as I make a small confession. As I mentioned in the Introduction, both of my grandfathers were mathematical people; one was an engineer, the other a finance wiz. Despite having these smart men in my gene pool, my parents hired more math tutors in school than anyone I know. I simply lacked the motivation to grow my mathematical competence. It wasn't until I started my company and was forced to pour over balance sheets that I developed my understanding of how key variables of equations unlock business breakthroughs.

You probably know even better than I do that if you can't properly organize and prioritize variables, you won't know how to approach an equation. Surprise—the same is true when it comes to communication: If you don't understand the key variables of presentations, you won't be able to unlock your effectiveness and advance your work.

Many speakers initiate the presentation preparation process with the wrong approach. Right away, they leap to *what* they are going to present. They begin their preparation process by sifting through old presentation decks and documents in a desperate search for bullet points to share. Let's refer to this part of the communication framework as *content*, which may be compared to software code.

There are others who falter from the get-go, immediately imagining themselves standing in front of a room (or Zoom audience) with all eyes upon them. Their nervous system reacts as if they are experiencing a bodily SEV0 (a catastrophic incident, such as a product bug that brings an app to a complete standstill). Their fight-or-flight responses kick in. Their faces flush while they fidget with their fingers, look down at their feet, sway back-and-forth, and fumble with meaningless filler words. Let's refer to this part of the communication framework as *delivery*, which might be likened to deploying code after it's been developed.

In later chapters, we'll discuss best practices for crafting compelling content and tips for delivering it confidently. Both of those elements are crucial, but only if they're considered with ample context; otherwise, they will be limited in their effectiveness and come across as selfish. The missing first step to becoming a luminary? *Empathetic effectiveness.*

Countless hours of work time end up wasted due to lackluster, pointless presentations because the speakers didn't understand the needs and wants of their audiences. Imagine how much time you'd save by avoiding unnecessary tangents during meetings and/or additional follow-ups if people engaged with presentations more efficiently. If you were to devote just a few minutes ahead of time to consider your participants—who they were and what they needed to know—and then make a few subtle adjustments, your calendar would miraculously declutter, and you'd have a lot more time to devote to your technical work. Simple preparation techniques such as this would move you closer to luminary status because you would be doing more of what you love and less of what you dread.

SIDECAR

Listen up! The best *speakers* are the best *listeners*. They conduct research in advance to find out what their audiences want to hear and then deliver that information to ensure that the time together is well-spent. Think of a speaker's role in terms of a wise, customer-centric product manager who learns and considers how features of a product could be used based on insights about an addressable market before the developers write and ship the code.

Let's revisit the earlier scenario in which I described how your manager asked you at the last minute to present at the All Hands meeting. What would be your initial reaction to the public speaking assignment below?

    ____ *I would start hacking slides together by ripping through all my old decks, documents, reports, and notes.*
    ____ *I would visualize myself stammering and screwing up.*
    ____ *I would contact my peers and ask for them to help.*
    ____ *I would wing it and hope for the best.*
    ____ *I would tell my manager that I just got food poisoning and will be out tomorrow.*

If you checked off one or more of the above, don't sweat it. You're heading in the right direction by reading this book. I'm confident you'll overcome the dread of presenting; you may even start to enjoy it.

Collect Support, Not Dust

The Hidden Figures referenced earlier in this chapter were luminaries not only because of their mathematical ability, but also because of how they persevered through the challenges of communicating their technical work to a largely adverse audience. In 1961, with segregation still being the norm in American society, their gender and skin color automatically placed them at a disadvantage in terms of their words being taken seriously in a high-pressure, high-profile work environment run primarily by white men. Additionally, most of their stakeholders didn't care about the details of space travel calculations; they just wanted assurance that the behind-the-scenes work would lead to success on the launch pad.

These four remarkable women *knew their audience*, understanding *who* they were and *how* to communicate to them. Instead of presuming that their stakeholders cared about *the means* (i.e., the computations), they realized that they were emotionally connected to *the ends* (i.e., the outcomes, including a successful launch and the resulting global victory). So, in addition to their technical brilliance, the Hidden Figures adapted their communication style to navigate a tough NASA audience. All their calculations would have been for naught if they had been unable to effectively get their messages across. Their deliberate communication excellence landed footprints on the surface of America's history and planted a flag of technical innovation that will be remembered forever.

Does any of this sound familiar to you in your work circumstances? Maybe you are great at solving status quo problems, but what would happen if you thought of a new breakthrough ML (machine learning) project with tremendous potential upside that challenges current thinking, yet would require a significant investment of data scientists and GPU resources? Would you know how to pitch it and collect enough support to set it in motion?

It's possible you are a different kind of technical leader, one who focuses on infrastructure stability and needs management to pay attention to help you prevent looming vulnerabilities. Are you able to raise enough awareness to convince people of the urgency of the problem and devote essential resources in time to solve the issue with minimal sustained damage?

If you are solid at execution but can't get people to listen to your thoughts and ideas, your work and career trajectory will ultimately suffer because you haven't been able to enable your stakeholders and decision-makers to comprehend *what* you are talking about and realize *why* it's so important. Ultimately, this lack of persuasion hinders your prgress while your innovative ideas move to the shelf with other passed-over projects to collect dust.

You don't have to take it from me. The Project Management Institute reports that one-third of all projects completely fail due to lack of communication, while over half suffer from budget risk and/

or disappointing outcomes for the same reason. This is tragic because most communication breakdowns in technical environments are entirely preventable.

Sympathetic Synergy

Sympathy can serve as a powerful tool for a speaker. I don't mean "feeling sorry" for audience members, but rather being able to listen to them and their pain points in advance so you know what content people want to hear and how they will be most receptive to it. During the preparation stage, you are honing basic listening skills to dramatically improve the chances of your messages being received the way you intended. Speakers who take the time to learn about their audience upfront and then adapt their content based on those insights are exponentially more successful because their personalized communication creates synergy with their listeners. It makes the information more pertinent, relatable, and entertaining, which means that audience members will make an even greater effort to absorb what you are saying and support your initiatives.

I've attended more than my fair share of All Hands meetings in which it was plain as day the speakers had zero sympathy for their audience, which is typically diverse and includes a wide range of roles and interests across orgs. All too often, the speakers came across like *beeps* of a dump truck heading in reverse, unloading mounds of unnecessary and boring technical details onto the attendees. When it was over, the messages were scattered amidst a wave of dusty, cluttered refuse.

Have you witnessed occasions in which your colleagues presented potential future work to their managers and stepped out of the meetings high-fiving their friends thinking they "nailed it!"?

Little did the engineers realize that they'd backed up their dump trucks. They became shocked one week later when they found out that their work wouldn't receive funding to continue for the following year. They scratched their heads, at a loss for what they did wrong. When they replayed the presentation in their minds, they realized that they had provided endless technical details of the ins and outs of the potential project but failed to provide topline messages in a relatable manner.

Don't get me wrong, I'm *not* against technical deep dives. I count myself as one of the strongest proponents of thorough explanations if they make sense with relevant information and are not overdone. It might make sense, for example, to back up the demo dump truck when you have an update with fellow domain experts who can help

---

SIDECAR

Realize that your work is always part of a bigger workflow. Your technical projects are typically smaller pieces of the broader business puzzle. Just like distributed systems, your projects and tools likely have many dependencies on other people's technical efforts. So, increase the likelihood of your siloed success by sympathizing with your stakeholders and broadening the appeal of your work. You can also check out Peter Senge's bestselling book, *The 5th Disciple*, to learn about systems thinking to drive higher productivity.

---

the group whiteboard a tough statistics problem. Another appropriate circumstance might involve showcasing how the company's new AI model has accelerated company growth with impressive technical prowess to build confidence in future ML endeavors.

To close my plea for more sympathy, let's imagine that you are a tourist riding a ferry under the Golden Gate bridge and are sitting next to the architect of the historic structure. (RIP to the actual the chief engineer, Joseph Strauss, who passed away in 1938.) After the two of you make small talk about sites to visit while in San Francisco, the architect chimes in with a barrage of details about the bridge, including intricate measurements of each sprawling crack and the calculations involved in determining the unreliability of the old materials used to support the arches that happened to be directly above you. Instead of enjoying the sights and view, all you can think about is a massive metal carrot crashing on your boat. You become so afraid of this possibility that you tune out everything else the architect says afterwards.

Is this example a bit exaggerated? Maybe. However, it's not far off from what typically happens when technical presenters—who are sometimes critical and pessimistic—get so caught up in their own language and belief systems that they fail to realize they have left their audiences drowning in the details. If the attendees haven't totally checked out, they are panicking about how the potential negative outcomes might impact their work and if they should be looking for another job.

To make the ferry ride less frightening and more inspiring, the architect could have identified his audience (casual tourists) prior to speaking and demonstrated some sympathy (i.e., recognize their lack of architectural awareness). If he had considered their limited interest in hearing the technical drawbacks about the bridge, the architect could have adjusted his comments and presented safety concerns in a more relatable way.

If you only take away one thing from this chapter, it's the fact that we don't determine the success of our communications: Our *audience* does. You need to understand them and their pain because, guess what, we're all a bit selfish. Your audience members primarily care about their work and how it's impacted by others, like you.

Recommendation Models

Every organization conducts meetings and presentations that are obligatory for respective groupings of employees. Unfortunately, some organization members attend because they don't feel they have a choice. This doesn't mean they have to pay attention, however. If the speakers selfishly focus on what they feel is interesting and/or important to them but fail to adapt and shine a light on why the work matters to the group, the effort will be a waste of time for everyone involved and dissolve in darkness.

Amazon, for example, is concentrated on what the consumer wants, not the other way around. Their AI recommendation models are designed to serve up products in the app that resemble what the customer has already purchased: "Customers who viewed items in your browsing history also viewed…" Similarly, Netflix tracks our binge watching habits and leverages our viewership data habits to suggest TV shows and films we might be interested in. Other usages of data aside, Amazon and Netflix are being customer-centric and sympathetic to our needs by saving us time searching for a product or show to watch. While not every recommendation will be accurate, for the most part consumers appreciate that these businesses are paying attention, care, and are at least trying to improve the experience.

When you prepare your presentations, do you consider relevant data about your audience? Will you be able to connect with their technical experiences when you share yours? Are you thinking in terms of what might inform as well as entertain?

Whether you're a hardware engineer, software developer, data scientist, or any other technical professional, you have a choice. You can spend your time heads down solving the same old problems with limited exposure of your work. Or you can become a luminary by shining light on certain aspects of problems that illuminate areas of personal relevance for your listeners, so they invite you to help with new problems. Unlike Relli from this book's Introduction, you can think about your presentation attendees in advance and determine what makes sense to share for a particular group, and what you can skip. In the next chapter, I'll provide practical tips for how to analyze and adapt to your audience, even if you have minimal time like a last-minute All Hands request from your manager, which will help earn your audience's trust as it shows that you *listened*, are *sympathetic*, and truly *appreciate* them.

The technical and societal legacy of the Hidden Figures women continues to make waves six decades later. But they would never have had a chance to change NASA—and the world—if they hadn't adapted to their difficult audience. Be aware that your attendees will always have a wide range of familiarity with your work. Some people will be more technical, whereas others less so. In both cases, they want content that is directly relevant *to them* and explained in a way that demonstrates sympathy to their situation.

Takeout

Before we move on to the next chapter, I want to close with a reference to the first wave of the 2020 COVID-19 pandemic, when takeout food orders skyrocketed by seventy percent.

As if it wasn't hard enough for restaurants during lockdown to deal with the difficulties of closed dining areas, delayed supply chains, and overwhelming cleaning regulations, they also had to cope with impatient customers who demanded warm meals to be ready for on-time pickup. Instead of serving tables full of people, restaurant workers had to package, bag, and organize meals in perfect order or risk receiving poor customer reviews online.

Similarly, we can think of our audience members as customers and ourselves as restaurant workers serving what they need to make sure we receive positive reviews about our technical work, which ultimately enables more customers. But just as restaurants face the danger of leaving customers with the wrong meal, we can leave our audiences with the wrong message.

I'll share more guidance for ending presentations on a strong note in Chapter Five, but for now I'll leave *you* with the simple tip to leave your audience with simple takeaways. I'll do this at the end of each chapter in this book, so you walk away from my counter with what you need. Like a good restaurant, the worker should tell you in a simple way what you're leaving with.

Imagine you went to pick up your takeout meal with a hangry

family waiting at home. Before the worker hands you the bag full of food, he dives into details: "Hi Alice, confirming you have four orders of our burger meal that has sesame buns with two circular patties, three different vegetables, and a variety of condiments, as well as fried potatoes with salt and cups full of two percent milk with Dreyer's vanilla ice cream that has been in our freezer for sixteen days."

I'll admit that I do appreciate seeing the details of my order on drive-thru screens, but if I have an impatient family at home waiting for me to pickup our takeout, I'd much prefer, "Here's your burger meals and shakes with a receipt in the bag if you want to confirm the details of your order." The same can apply to an All Hands presentation, or any other time you present to a diverse group of audience members. In both instances, audiences and consumers likely have some degree of impatience because they're busy and want to keep moving, so leave them with key takeaways to make sure they keep your main message in mind.

Takeaways
- Recognize that the fear of public speaking is the root cause of physiological symptoms that plague nervous presenters.

- Overcome fear and avoid anxiety about presentations by taking ample time to prepare based on insightful context.

- Contextual preparation begins with orienting our communications around our audience because they determine the success of our technical presentations.

- Research shows that content delivered in a customized fashion earns better attention and engagement with audiences.

- Maximize engagement with audience members by serving them with sympathy and succinct takeaways.

CHAPTER TWO

Adapt to Audiences—Part Two

When Marissa Mayer took the helm at Yahoo, the organization was a far cry from its legendary origins in 1995 when Jerry Lang and David Filo created a massive digital index dubbed "Jerry and David's Guide to the Worldwide Web" and their profits soared until they faced headwinds. The company struggled against rising competitive threats from newcomers such as Google and, prior to Marissa's arrival in 2012, experienced a revolving door of CEOs, with five in the same number of years.

Marissa had her hands full taking the reins of a business suffering from diminishing returns and a deflated culture. She knew she had to leverage learnings from Google's success and prioritize people by instating the company-wide All Hands meeting that I mentioned in the Introduction. At that time in 2012, I happened to be working as a contractor on the Yahoo events team and we scraped together the first weekly All Hands meeting (called "FYI"), which led to a defining moment in my career: Marissa personally approved my FTE (full time employee) hiring packet, which led me to spearhead the FYI initiative for over five years. In this role, I had the opportunity to work with an incredible variety of 1,300+ speakers—ranging from interns to CTOs—all of whom wanted to best represent their team's work when they took the Sunnyvale headquarters stage and spoke in front of what was primarily a technical audience.

To produce top quality content, I had to constantly remind these speakers that their audience was comprised of at least *some* attendees who weren't nearly at their level of expertise. It was then I became drawn to my deeper calling as a coach and trainer who sought to bridge the gap between technical speakers and their stakeholders. I'm forever grateful to my fellow "purple-bleeding Yahoos" who supported my calling and helped me find my way as I stumbled through my early career, which eventually led to the formation of LUV.

Along my entrepreneurial journey, I've often thought of luminaries, such as Jerry Yang and David Filo, who were onto something when they started their online directory as a *guide* to the worldwide web." If it hadn't been for them and some particularly supportive senior leaders such as Marissa Mayer, I wouldn't have embraced the call to become a guide and encourage speakers to do the same. In this chapter, I will take my in-the-trenches experience and teach *you* how to become a more trusted *guide* for your listeners by sharing a map with directions to help you navigate the obstacles to audience engagement.

SIDECAR

Good presentations are like accordions. They expand and contract by alternating between shorter and lengthier sections of content to keep audiences engaged with varying amounts of explanation. To model this principle, we'll follow the previous chapter–which was a bit shorter–by now expanding with breadth to cover a variety of practical tips for understanding and engaging your audiences.

---

34   Luminary

How Hidden Figures Achieved the Impossible

Prior to achieving their mathematical breakthroughs at NASA, the Hidden Figures women began their journey toward luminosity at NACA (the National Advisory Committee for Aeronautics), where they took on many demanding projects with significant organizational obstacles. Their technical achievements were nothing short of magnificent, but the truly impressive part was *how* they achieved their results. Back in the 1950s, they didn't have fancy mainframes to run automated algorithms to solve statistical problems for them. They were *human computers* long before the existence of calculators. Instead of being able to type in commands and equations, they were limited to basic tools such as rulers, paper, and pencils to evaluate and dissect aeronautical equations. Our heroines recognized the power of analyzing variables, which led to their ability to adapt to the problems before solving them.

The importance of adapting to our audiences is a critical key to unlocking successful storytelling. But the idea remains *untapped knowledge* unless it is *applied* and then transformed into *wisdom*.

Whether earlier in my coaching career at Yahoo, or more recently while leading Light Up Ventures, the pattern has remained the same: Presenters who ignore their audience get ignored when they present. This pitfall can easily be avoided if they take their audiences into account right from the start of their presentation preparation. The Hidden Figures women were successful in this regard because their proper analysis of variables upfront enabled them to *adapt* findings for their audiences later. The same holds true regarding presentations. By analyzing our audiences at an early stage, we can adapt to them because we know exactly *what* to share—and *not* share—with them. You work hard on your technical problems, and you should work just as hard to make sure your presentations about your work will resonate with your stakeholders, or the entire presentation will fall flat and be a waste of time for all concerned.

The challenge: How do we identify in advance what will resonate? Let's start by addressing basic facts about audiences today…

Cognitive Overload

Any speaker is already at a disadvantage before she or he takes the stage (or shares their screen on Zoom). It just takes a quick skim of the statistics to know what we are up against when it comes to the average American's mindshare:

- Exposed to 50,000 advertisements per week.

- Spends two and a half hours per day on social media.

- Checks email thirty-six times per hour.

As if the above isn't enough, a recent study found that businesses lose $650 billion every year due to distractions—from advertisements to entertainment to our increasing dependence on devices. Distractions are devastating to individuals, organizations, and the economy in terms of daily productivity. Yet most people don't consider how much time is also wasted from unsuccessful presentations. First, there is the impact on the audiences who miss the point of the discussion because the speaker didn't communicate well. Second, there are the speakers themselves who lost countless hours gearing up for the presentation, rambling for hours in front of indifferent participants, and answering all the follow-up questions to things that should have been clear during the presentation.

Don't believe me? Think about the last team meeting you attended and estimate the percentage of comments you retained. Or, being honest with yourself, admit to all the multitasking you did while you were on your last Zoom call.

I'm not suggesting that you beat yourself up for any of this. It's human nature and how we're wired. Neuroscience proves that our brains love distractions, especially ones that excite us and trigger rushes of dopamine (the neurotransmitter that sends signals to our pleasure centers).

The greatest enemy of presenters is *cognitive overload*—when a system's capacity can't handle the overwhelming amount of information it receives. Our brains, like data storage machines, have capacity limits. Remember Relli from the previous chapter? His visitors dropped off the tour due to cognitive overload, a situation that could have been averted.

Be aware that your audience members have limitations on the amount of information they can handle, especially if they aren't as technical as you are. Nobody understands your work as much as you do. They can't help being distracted about other priorities as they listen to you present, especially if you are backing up the dump truck of technical overload on them.

Your role as speaker is to meet your audience where they are in regard to their familiarity and interest in your work. This involves earning their trust and grabbing their attention right away, delivering on their expectations, and steering clear of unnecessary minutiae that might confuse and/or bore them. If you accomplish this, you can prevent the audience members from seeking out distractions by helping them focus on content that is relevant and well-organized. When analyzing the variables of your audience, consider what they're capable of processing, so they can understand your work more easily, and therefore, better support your ideas. To land the point, remember that your audience rarely cares as much about your work as you do, which means you should consider the classic quote from Jerry McGuire: "Help me help you!"

The Audience in Capes and Spandex

You've no doubt heard the cliché that imagining your audience in their underwear helps overcome stage jitters. The concept is that the image is so ludicrous that it makes you relax and feel less intimidated by your audience. Do I think the guidance is helpful? No. I think it's creepy and may be detrimental to your presentation. It's disrespectful to think of people this way, as you lose sight of *who* they are, *what* they want from you, and *how* you impart information to them.

I have a different idea if you'd like to imagine your audience dressed in anything other than their current outfits: Envision them as superheroes wearing capes. Whether the individuals are your teammates, users of your technical services, external stakeholders, or a mix of all the above, it's best to think of them as people who deserve your respect and the best you have to offer. By positioning them as heroes, you will never come across as condescending. Instead, you'll embody a mentality of servant leadership because you are providing them with helpful information. There is also a better chance that you will take greater pains to ensure that you are presenting *what* they want to know and *how* they want to hear it.

Simplify, Simplify

At the risk of overplaying the underwear motif and oversharing, I admit that most of my underwear is the same color and material. Why should you care? The answer is simple: Having one color makes the underwear easy for me to remember and identify amongst the heaps of laundry that pile up in my house full of kids. Recognition helps with efficiency, turning daily tasks—such as getting ready for the day—into rote processes that gives me back precious time for things that are more beneficial and, hopefully, memorable. It also opens a bit more room in a crowded, overloaded subconscious mind to focus on things that truly matter. It's the same logic behind why Albert Einstein wore similar-looking gray suits every day and

Steve Jobs—who could certainly have afforded to wear anything he wanted—often chose to wear the same trademark black turtleneck in public.

Eighteenth century philosopher Henry David Thoreau famously said, "Our life is frittered away by detail…simplify, simplify." We've already established that, while our audience members are superheroes, they are lazy and distracted when it comes to paying attention and absorbing new concepts. Simplifying your presentation to just the metaphorical "black underwear" (or whatever color you happen to prefer) means providing content that is easily *familiar* to people and therefore most understandable because it enables efficient recognition. The more foreign (unfamiliar) the information, the harder it becomes for you to grab and sustain their attention because you are forcing them to devote increased focus and mindpower on what you are trying to communicate. Simple and recognizable messages will always make your audience more receptive to what you intend to share.

Slow to Speak, Quick to Listen

Now let's tackle how to best understand your heroic audience: *analysis*. By this, I'm referring to how you can dig deep to understand your audience members and then adapt your communications accordingly.

When you boil it down, what does a professional therapist do best in order to help their patients? *Listen* to her or his patient. Similarly, a speaker must learn to become a masterful listener to learn about her or his audience, analyze the research, become sympathetic—a major component we established in Chapter One—and produce a personalized presentation to help solve for the pain points of their audience. In the noisy outside world with so many constant distractions, this can be quite a challenge.

Think about a recent conversation you had. Did you maintain eye contact throughout, zero in on every word, process what was said, acknowledge the meaning, and pay attention to the person's wellbeing? Probably not. More likely, you picked up a few pieces here and there but, chances are your mind wandered to other things, and you glanced at your phone a few times. Or perhaps you tried to focus on the other party with good intentions, but you were concentrating so hard on your follow-up statement or question that you missed a few things along the way.

It's important for you to realize that while people are sometimes looking for a two-sided conversation, often they aren't. On many occasions, people *just want to be heard*. This involves a lot more than you might think. It's not enough to simply acknowledge the message; you must communicate back to the speaker that you truly heard and understood it to gain full connection. This involves a practice known as *active listening* in which you:

1. Listen intently.

2. Process what's being said.

3. Repeat the words back to the speaker to be sure you grasped the statement and meaning.

4. Reflect on and respond to what's being said.

5. Store the information for later use.

Active listening not only supports effective communication, but it also helps you develop sympathetic attunement that helps you form a relationship bond. Think of it like a radio antenna that is picking up signals enabling you to hit the right frequency when you impart content to them during your presentation. As Nancy Duarte, author of the powerful book *Resonate*, recommends: "The audience does not need to tune themselves to you—you need to tune your message to them. Skilled presenting requires you to understand their hearts and minds and create a message to resonate with what's already there."

You're now ready for the three steps involved in analyzing your audience, which I've affectionately named *moccasin motivation, rest stops,* and *binary blazing.*

Moccasin Motivation

As discussed in the previous chapter, thinking about what's important to others will help you attain what's important to you. So, you're probably wondering, how do moccasins fit in?

One of the beautiful things about moccasins is that you don't have to tie laces to be able to walk in them for several miles. The same is true when it comes to imagining what your audience members think and feel. When you slip into their metaphorical moccasins, it becomes easier for you to figure out the underlying motivation behind why they are showing up to hear you. Is it a standard organizational All Hands meeting? Did they register to hear your conference tech talk on a particular subject? Everyone expects to gain something in exchange for their time and attention. Simply ask yourself: *Why is my audience here and how can I adapt by giving them what they want?*

Rest Stops

Once you've processed the thoughts and feelings of your audience members, you are then ready to support them on their journeys. Keep in mind that everyone has an individual path on which she or he is pursuing professional and/or personal progress. As presenters, we can provide attendees with tools to accelerate their journeys while also offering a diversion, a change of pace from their same-old daily grind.

Think of your presentation as a timely rest stop where people can engage with you and become nourished and energized. You are providing expert knowledge and technical solutions for them to chew on, digest, and process. You aren't pressuring them to do exactly what you tell them, but rather, helping shine a light on things they might not have thought of before, like a travel brochure of interesting local hot spots that might be perused over a much-needed cup of coffee.

As the audience's tour guide, you can address the group from the start and demonstrate sympathy by asking them for a show of hands to basic, relatable questions:

- How many of you are here because you are struggling to integrate the new database system?

- Who here is frustrated with AI models that lack fresh data?

- How many of you are snot happy about the recent migration?

- Who here doesn't understand the new coding language requirements?

The above are just examples, of course, and should be tailored to suit your specific topics. Once you've seen how many people have raised their hands to each question, you can glean insights into their needs, wants, and pain points and then address them accordingly.

Soliciting audience reactions also demonstrates how much you care, as you are asking for their input and opinions. The rest falls upon you to adapt and deliver on those expectations, which proves that you heard them (active listening).

Binary Blazing

Suppose you are on a long, complicated drive on an unfamiliar highway that doesn't have a strong enough signal for GPS. You pay close attention to every road sign, so you don't miss your exit or head in the wrong direction. If the signs above are cluttered with numerous words and arrows on them and you are racing seventy miles per hour, you are likely to feel overwhelmed and misread or misunderstand the language and where you should (or shouldn't) go.

When it comes to making a technical presentation, your audience is either going to be receptive to a lot of jargony details or not. Simplify your audience analysis with a binary understanding of their composition:

1. *Fellow SMEs (subject matter experts):* The individuals who have familiarity with your work and are likely to be interested in the details, including the *how* behind the solutions to technical problems.

2. *Indirect Stakeholders:* The people who primarily care about the impact of the work, not *how* it was achieved. They are most interested in the *what* and *why*. This group of professionals includes senior leaders, cross-functional stakeholders, customers, etc.

You have the potential to win over an audience simply by knowing which grouping your audience falls into and catering to their preferences. If attendees are fellow SMEs, you can feel comfortable incorporating deep technical details into your presentation, depending on their level of technical understanding. Consider their motivation for attendance. Are they looking to solve a problem or break through a roadblock? Do they want tips on how to do their jobs faster or better?

If, however, they are primarily senior leaders, you need to be mindful of their subject matter familiarity or you risk offering content that goes over their heads or bores them to the point of tuning out. The individuals who fall into this grouping usually just want the top-line (or bottom-line) information. Do they need to know if the product launch date is on track? Are they concerned about the project going over budget? Have you discovered new product features that could potentially be monetized? In each of these examples, a simple explanation is all that is required; the leaders don't need to know as much about *how* you kept the project on track or *how* you figured out the computations that led you to come up with a valuable idea.

Deeper Analysis

Our training participants are often surprised when I inform them that neither they nor their products or services are the main considerations for their presentations. As I hope I've already made clear, *your audience members are the heroes*. It's not about you or your offerings, no matter how wonderful they may be. You are merely there to serve as a guide on their journeys to help them learn something new or overcome a challenge. You'll learn more about "the Hero's Journey" in Chapter Six, where I share practical guidance about crafting content with proven frameworks for successful storytelling. For now, identifying your audience members as heroes enables you to leverage the three powerful "modes of persuasion" identified by ancient Greek philosopher Aristotle in his work *Rhetoric*:

- *Logos:* This word translates to "reason." The audience is always looking for the speaker to be logical with a rationale appeal based on facts with reputable sources that support statements. Technical audiences appreciate clear-cut communication with minimal hand-wavey fluff to enable maximum engagement.

- *Ethos:* This word translates to "character." When it comes to public speaking, character is reflected by how much *credibility* the speaker brings to the subject. This might involve several things, including one's ability to bring appropriate credentials, expertise, and relevant knowledge to the table.

- *Pathos:* This word translates to "suffering" and "experience." Pathos focuses on the human element involved in the subject matter. The speaker always needs to connect on an emotional level with the audience by considering how their content will make audience members feel.

All three of the above modes of persuasion—which we'll cover in-depth in Chapter Four—must be thoughtfully considered for a speaker to effectively "persuade" attendees to her or his point of view and/or approach. A lack of credibility, logic, or an emotional connection can produce disastrous results between a speaker and audience that is difficult to recoup once things have gone off course.

With the modes of persuasion in mind, let's continue our options for audience analysis by considering a few high-level questions:

- *What do your audience members desire?*

- *What are their wants vs. needs related to your presentation?*

- *What makes them tick?*

- *What could be in the way of your audience supporting your work?*

- *What is the right balance of higher-level storytelling and technical detail?*

The above questions will jumpstart things to help you understand your group. Now I'm going to throw a curveball your way: What if the audience consists of a *range* of attendees? While your attendees share the common interest of attending your presentation, their interests and motivations could be quite diverse. To avoid the danger of homogenizing your audience, recognize that every presentation is as unique as the individuals watching it, which means you should plan to address different sub-segments with targeted messages throughout your presentation. To do so, consider your analysis of your presentation attendees and assess whether you can break them into a few key groups and then present relevant messages to each accordingly. Maybe one group consists of fellow SMEs whereas another is less aware of your project, so you'd want to prepare a few subsections of content that appeal to both groups with a balance of technical depth and high-level context.

Now we're ready to dig a bit deeper in our audience analysis by considering their needs, wants, and aspirations. This is where Maslow's Hierarchy may be a useful tool to consider.

The pyramid prioritizes basic human needs in order, from bottom to top: physiological (air, food, water, shelter, clothing, sleep); safety and security (health, career, property, family); love and belonging (family, friendship, intimacy); self-esteem (confidence, individualism, achievement); and self-actualization (morality, purpose, creativity,

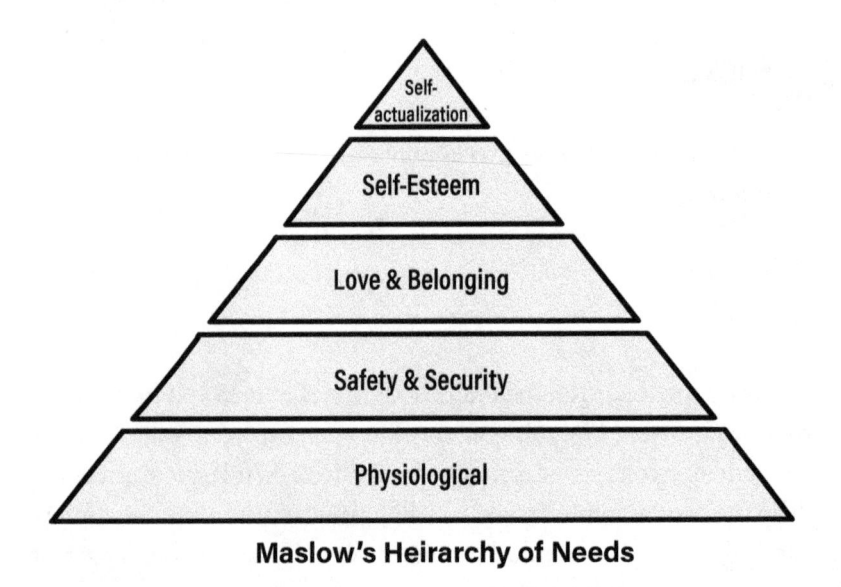

Maslow's Heirarchy of Needs

spontaneity, acceptance). While your presentation may help your listeners feel secure about your technical contributions, you'll mostly want to focus on the top three groups of needs. Below are few thought starters to help you understand how your presentations can appeal to the needs of your audience:

- For *belonging*, you might appeal to team members' desire to feel involved by presenting opportunities for collaboration with your project that facilitate a sense of contribution and personal connection.

- For *self-esteem*, you can simply acknowledge any members in your audience who supported the success of your work and appeal to their individual need for recognition. Humbly calling out joint achievement from fellow contributors earns respect from your audience members.

- For *self-actualization*, you can up-level the perceived impact of your work by creatively presenting how your technical accomplishments supported broader business success. For example, mentioning the purpose of your data pipeline as a catalyst for better user experience with your company's apps will help your audience realize and accept the broader value of your work.

Before we close this chapter with a few final tips for analyzing your audience, let's consider the following questions to increase precision with understanding your *who*:

- *What is their level of awareness with your content?* If the attendees are veteran members of your team and/or are experts on the subject, you can speak at a lower level and don't have to be concerned with the depth of details. If, however, the audience consists of people from another department, new members, are part of a new cross-functional group, you'll need to simplify things, skip excessive technical details, and avoid intimidating-sounding acronyms and jargon.

- *What is their level of interest?* This requires careful thought and objectivity. You may think everyone is going to be interested in everything you have to say, but such presumptions can be deadly to a presentation. If you are one hundred percent certain they have bought in to your concepts, then be as concise as possible. If most of the audience is in the dark about your topic or in some way skeptical about what you must present, you'll need to cook up some persuasive soup with ethos, logos, and pathos to win them over.

- *What is their business level?* If you're speaking to executives, your main order of business is to focus on the big picture and measurable impact. These are people who don't have time to waste, so present top-line information only. You should avoid barraging them with technical information, even if it seems interesting to you or you think it "proves" your case. You can always inform them you will answer questions later and provide more detail if they want it. By contrast, when you communicate with your peers, they might appreciate technical insights; in fact, they might want to see as much evidence to support your points as you can provide. Often you are rallying the troops to support a collaborative initiative; if this is the case, be specific about asks and follow-ups. Lastly, don't forget to consider any unfortunate politics that might be involved with reporting structures among your attendees and any organizational nuances involved.

- *What risk versus reward is at stake for them?* Think about the potential upsides and pressures involved for your attendees. Is there revenue, time, workload, or staffing involved in what you are presenting? If the initiative you propose means greater revenue and growth, then you have plenty of reward incentives to dangle in front of them. However, if it involves more work or cutbacks, tread delicately and put yourself in their shoes, as some of your content might come across as threatening.

In addition to contextual questions about your audience, there are always logistical factors that must be considered:

- *What season is it?* During certain times of year—notably summer and end-of-year holidays—many people suffer from *holi-daze*, meaning they are crazed with shorter-than-usual attention spans as they gear up for time off. You can counter this by being extra intentional with the amount of information you're sharing and use hyper-concise messaging. You can also preview projects that will take off after the holiday lull and let your audience know that you'll follow up with a deeper dive when everyone returns from vacation. However, if you're presenting during the spring or fall when many projects are full speed ahead, you can offer technical deep dives, product roadmaps, progress updates, obstacles to launch, calls to action, and budget/staffing needs.

- *Are you presenting after lunchtime?* If so, think about whether your group might be heading into an afternoon lull. This is a good opportunity for you to raise the energy level by inviting everyone to stand up, stretch, and refill on caffeine.

- *Is the presentation in-person, virtual, or both?* I'll share delivery tips for virtual presentations in Chapter Eight, but for now, be aware that your audience members may be even more distracted if they're tuning in virtually. You may want to consider a balance of sharing your screen to show slides while frequently taking a break from them to maintain human connection with the people on screen. If the presentation is in person, after lunch, and/or during a busy season, consider asking your audience questions throughout your talk to infuse more discussion and opportunities to re-engage along the way.

Measure and Modify

When my team is asked to provide a group training to improve an organization's communication skills, we always conduct pre-assessments to ensure we understand the cohort, so we can customize our core curriculum to their specific needs. As much as I love geeking out on the quantitative benchmark metrics (1-10 ratings of their skill levels) from the pre-assessments that we send to trainees, the gold is found in the qualitative measurement. In addition to the skill-level ratings, we ask participants to respond to the following:

- *Who is your typical presentation audience?*

- *What are the challenges you face when communicating with that audience?*

- *What type of content do you typically present to your audience?*

- *What do you most enjoy presenting that demonstrates your passion?*

- *What suggestions do you have that would make our training most useful to you?*

The responses to the questions above allow my team to customize our training curriculum to deliver a more personalized experience that ultimately drives higher improvement ratings for the quantitative benchmarks. This approach can also help you assess your audience members. If you're speaking at a conference, ask the organizers to provide you with any data points they have about the attendees. If you don't have formal access to such data, do your best to answer my sample questions from above and make your slides as relevant to your audience as possible.

Now that you've asked and considered analytical questions to better understand your audience, the last step in the preparation process is to synthesize all the data points into a succinct summary of your audience insights. This one bullet point, which briefly describes your audience, should appear at the top of your speaker notes under each of your slides. After this has been drafted, go through the slides to determine which ones will resonate with that identified audience. If one doesn't, either adjust the messaging or skip it for that presentation but save it for another one where it might be better suited to another audience.

Immediate Insights

At this stage, you may be thinking, *Great questions, Jack, but I don't have enough time for all this analytical work.*

If this is the case, I've provided a quick script below that can help you address a smaller audience and engage them in dialogue at the start of your presentation to glean immediate insights about them. Presentations that open things up to discussion have a better chance of keeping the audience engaged because attendees are forced to pay attention and participate from the start. If you don't have time to analyze your audience but want to ensure your information is relevant, begin your meeting with this simple script to gain immediate insights:

Hello, I'm prepared to present XX (brief, high-level heading about your technical topic) to accomplish XX (briefly define objectives of the meeting/presentation). Before I go any further, I want to make this a good use of everyone's time, so I'd like to pause here and ask, "What else would you like me to cover? Is there anything else I should know before I share my slides?

By stating your purpose upfront and then fielding questions, you are demonstrating that you are prepared to be flexable based on their comments. This approach also provides you with potential insights you can incorporate on the fly, ensuring that your content is as relevant as possible while also avoiding a common pitfall with presentations: *tangents.* How often have you labored over preparing your slides, yet only made it halfway through them because your audience asked irrelevant questions or made distracting comments that ate up presentation time? The above script will help field and flag potential detours and keep you in the driver's seat of your presentations.

Sometimes people will ask you to cover topics that are outside the scope of your presentation and chew up time better spent on your core content. That's not to say the requests are irrelevant and should be dismissed. You can acknowledge the suggestion and say you will try to cover it at the end, assuming there is enough time left. If it simply can't be done, say, "Thanks for so much for bringing that up. I agree, it's important. Unfortunately, we only have an hour to spend here and a lot of material to cover. Perhaps we put that in the parking lot for now and schedule a follow-up at a later date?"

The Most Important Person in the Room

I'll let you take a guess about the individual you think is "the most important person in the room" during your presentation. I'll give you a hint, it most certainly isn't you.

The most important attendee is...*drum roll*...the *decision maker* (or plural if there happens to be more than one). Most often, this is the senior leader(s) responsible for strategic decisions. However, there are some anti-hierarchal tech companies that have cultures in which the technical leads are empowered to make efficient decisions. Whoever must sign off on the strategy, the next steps, the budget, or any actionable feedback for things to move forward is the person you should be most focused on during your presentations. There are some practical approaches you can take that will help tilt her or his attention in your favor. We already mentioned the big one: Hover around top-line information—the broader technical implications, timeline considerations, strategic benefits, etc.—and avoid backing up the dump truck of deep technical refuse.

Another tip for engaging the decision maker (DM) is to mimic her or his posture and/or expression to improve connection (without overdoing it and seeming like you are mocking them, of course). The DM can set the tone for you and, in turn, the rest of the audience. If the DM has a serious demeanor and expression, you should do the same and lean in to demonstrate a down-to-business sentiment. If, however, the presentation is a casual brainstorm and the DM seems to be in a relaxed mood, the tone of your presentation can be somewhat lighter with more white space for discussion. In either scenario, my guidance is to avoid going to any extremes: Behavior that is overly serious or too flippant will have an adverse reaction.

Let's revisit the hypothetical scenario of the boat ride with the architect of the Golden Gate Bridge from the previous chapter. If the gentleman had known that his fellow riders on the boat consisted of potential financial donors to support his bridge work, he may have taken a bit more time to listen instead of spewing out technical information.

The same may be said of Relli. If he had known upfront that senior leaders and product managers were among his tour group, he would have avoided barraging his stakeholders with technical minutiae. Instead, he would have focused on the topline innovations and benefits—the *what* and *why*, not as much about the *how*—and probably had a fully engaged group who would remain with him until the end.

Tough Crowd

As I was writing this chapter, I received an email from my friends in Haiti about potential violent riots taking place there the following week. Unfortunately, this is the same story that had been ongoing in this country long before my first trip there in 2016.

Since then, I've returned to Haiti nine times. Each trip has been an adventure story in and of itself. If there were riots taking place when we landed, my fellow travelers and I would cover our faces with our jackets as we drove from the airport in Port-au-Prince to safe houses. Things have only continued to worsen in Haiti, especially since the mysterious assassination of their prime minister in 2020, along with devastating natural disasters, COVID-19, and gang violence which have left the country in shambles.

Given the increased unrest, we started flying into the relatively safer city of Cap Haitian in the North to bypass the road blockades of burning tires from people protesting their horrific situations. It didn't take long for Cap Haitian to also become unsafe with gang violence and kidnappings, so my group started flying from Florida on an old puddle jumper war plane into a small town where we land on a recently mowed field where our contacts graciously welcome us with warm smiles despite their dire circumstances.

You're probably wondering, *All right, Jack, what's the point? What does this have to do with adapting to my audience?*

My point is that no matter how cheerful and professional you are or what innocuous subject you are going to discuss, there is always a chance that you might have to deal with one or more difficult people in your audience. Some might be resentful and seek to thwart your plans with blockades of resistance in the form of firing challenging comments and questions, or some may just be having a bad day that is causing them to disengage with your presentation. It doesn't matter that you did nothing to trigger these behaviors. You need to take the high road, not react to or engage in any disputes, and avoid getting flustered. Your best bet is to fly right over any topics that might detract from your message.

If you are ever faced with a hot head who is out to disrupt your presentation with snide comments or provocative questions, while maintaining your composure you can politely respond by maintaining your composure and saying something like, "Thanks for the passionate comment. It sounds like you'd like to know more about the topic I shared. For the sake of everyone else in the room, I'm going to move on to my next subject, but I am happy to follow up with you separately when I finish my presentation."

Engineering audiences can sometimes be critical. Many love to nitpick about mistakes, challenge your theories, and shoot holes in your presentation to expose potential problems. Try not to let these folks get under your skin, reduce your enthusiasm, or dampen your warmth.

At the same time, if a technical group is being relatively quiet, don't overly read into their stoic expressions and make false assumptions. It's entirely possible that they are simply concentrating as they process your content. I've wrongly assumed by the expressionless faces of attendees at my talks that people were disengaged, only to discover afterwards that they were deeply intrigued by my presentations and had tons of interesting follow-up questions.

> **SIDECAR**
>
> *Read the room!* If you're up against a stoic crowd of expressionless attendees, find a few friendly faces that seem engaged with your presentation based on their smiles, note-taking, or head nods. You will find comfort and confidence by focusing on them to help overcome the apparent disengagement of the other attendees.

Death Star Cheat Code

Imagine Luke Skywalker flying his T-65 X-wing star fighter jet through the tight tunnels of the Death Star before sniping the bullseye that blows up the evil monstrosity. Prior to his risky flight, he and his compatriot pilots had studied plans of the target, so they were well prepared to encounter the variables of the environment.

It's not all that different when it comes to preparing your presentation. You can achieve incredible breakthroughs with your audience (okay, hopefully you won't be blowing anything up) if you take sufficient time to analyze attendees, identify what's most important to them, and then deliver specific, well-crafted messages (the metaphorical X-wing fighter torpedoes) that strike dead center. (Don't worry, we'll cover how to craft precise talking points in Chapter Five.)

That said, you may be so strapped for time that it's not possible to do all the required research on your audience. If this is the case, I'm going to provide you with my "Death Star Cheat Code" that breaks your presentation into simple sections with weighted percentages for an idea of how to balance your content based on your audience:

- *Introduction:* Fifteen percent of the presentation to hook the audience's attention, explain necessary context, and build up a problem(s) before transitioning to the middle of your talk that explains how you solved the problem.

- *Middle:* Seventy-five percent of the presentation to convey the main messages of your presentation, which can be broken into sub-sections:

    ◊ Leverage the rule of three by organizing your subsections around three key takeaways.

    ◊ The technical depth across and within each sub-section should be proportional to the percentage breakdown of your audience—i.e., if sixty to seventy percent of the audience is technical, then two-thirds of the middle sub-sections should dive into the details.

- *Close*: Ten percent of the presentation. Here you are landing the plane by wrapping up succinctly with results from the technical work explained in the middle section, summarizing with key takeaways, and sharing brief comments about future work to build forward momentum.

Now that we've established the ins and outs of adapting to your audience, you are ready to soar to Elon Muskian heights of success as you learn the *what* and *why* of orienting around objectives.

Takeaways

- The best communicators are the best listeners.

- Analyze your audience at an early stage to help identify exactly what to share—and not share—with them.

- Avoid presenting your audience with information overload.

- Practice active listening before and during your

presentation to better cater to their needs (based on Maslow's hierarchy).

- Utilize the three powerful modes of persuasion: *ethos, logos,* and *pathos.*

- Identify and engage the decision maker (or makers) to expedite the progress of your work.

CHAPTER THREE

Orient Around Objectives—Part One

If you have bought in on the importance of prioritizing your audience at this point, your net communications worth has already come a long way since you first opened this book. While we are on the subject of "coming a long way," it's worth noting how much progress NASA has made since the Human Computers helped launch John Glenn into orbit. Additionally, Elon Musk's company, SpaceX, has rocketed private space exploration into a new dimension with 375 launches (all but three were mission successes) between 2010 and mid-August 2024.

An effective launch means the SpaceX team has achieved their specific purpose—whether placing satellites in strategic locations for Starlink connectivity in a new country or expanding the world's understanding of deep space. SpaceX has been remarkably efficient, lean, and economical with their efforts as well, due to exceptional innovation, planning, and execution.

In this chapter, we'll explore one of the primary reasons luminaries such as Musk have been remarkably successful in their innovative endeavors: their relentless determination to define and focus on the right goals. Whether you like the guy or not, it's tough to argue that he hasn't changed the world with disruptive luminosity while doing the technical work that he loves with hyper effectiveness.

Luminaries obsess over objectives, so they don't waste anyone's time (especially their own). Musk personally earns $6,887 per minute, which translates to nearly $10 million per day, and $69.4 million per week. How does he accomplish this extraordinary feat? Every meeting he attends is laser-focused on objectives. You can't launch rockets willy-nilly. The same holds true for delivering a presentation: You must know your *why* to not only effectively engage your audience, but also to ensure they rally behind your ideas and act upon your recommendations.

How often have you walked out of someone else's meeting wondering: *What was the point of that? What a waste of time!* You are way too busy with your daily technical work to throw away a second of precious time attending a pointless presentations. Now put on the moccasins we discussed in the previous chapter and think about the *participants* who attend *your* meetings. Yes, I specifically refer to them as participants, because they are not innocent bystanders who have time to spare. They're *active attendees* because they are looking for you to clearly demonstrate how your work and content directly impact them. When audiences listen to you, they are investing their time. It's your job to deliver valuable ROI (return on investment) by providing meaningful meetings in exchange for their attendance.

The takeaway: Don't waste your time creating a slapdash presentation slide deck that lacks purpose. Respect your time and theirs by defining objectives upfront and then delivering on them succinctly. If you can shave just a few minutes of presentation time and perhaps even end your meetings a few minutes early, your level of respect will move up and to the right.

Culture of Clarity

During my time working with Marissa Mayer on Yahoo's company-wide All Hands meetings, I dreaded witnessing technical speakers who failed to orient their content around specific objectives. It was painful for me knowing that these individuals had missed out on critical opportunities to showcase their teams' expertise and accomplishments.

Marissa knew full well from her time at Google with Larry Page and Sergey Brin the importance of creating a "culture of clarity." Establishing a clear company vision, purpose, values, and goals opens the door to strong communication, which leads to innovation and results. The same is true for a presenter on stage: Clarity is everything. If you effectively message your purpose right up front and deliver on it during the presentation without veering off-course, you will find that your ideas and initiatives will be well-received with many fewer follow-up questions from confused attendees.

SIDECAR

Once you understand your *who*, you can move on to your *why*, so that you may then create your *what* and deliver it effectively with your *how*.

Warm Connection

I live in the mountains with my family. One of my favorite pastimes is sipping a rich medium roast coffee while chatting with my wife next to our wood burning stove. I relish our deep conversations and have learned that two of the main ingredients for developing rich connections are *uninterrupted time* and a *warm environment* (both in terms of temperature and tone). It's difficult to explore people's dreams, opportunities, challenges, and pains if there are interruptions or if someone feels cold.

To craft the right environment for our stove-side conversations, I must plan ahead because wood stoves require more advance attention in advance than you might think. For starters, I must already have the right balance of kindling and logs in place. This means chopping the trees on my property ahead of time, allowing them to season for at least twelve months, and then stacking and replenishing them as needed.

Early in the morning, before carving out time to catch up with my wife, I begin the process of producing an efficient fire that will rage on its own with a domino effect of logs efficiently burning through each other. To start, I collect the logs from my seasoned stack, arrange them in the stove with great precision, and then light the base. Before the stove can become fully flaming with a palpable, earthy warmth, I must generate glowing hot embers below to fuel the flaming logs above. This involves frequently restacking and stoking the wood until the stove box is fully firing on all cylinders.

I go through this arduous process before my wife arrives, so I don't have to constantly get up and adjust the stove during our conversation. Sometimes I wonder if all this meticulous preparation and thoughtful execution is worth so much effort. But then I think about the extraordinary benefit: These conversations fuel our relationship and enable us to live our best lives.

You are probably wondering what my intimate wood stove conversations have to do with the subject of this book. You'd be surprised to know that they share a great deal in common. When my wife and I are in front of that fire discussing a wide range of topics, we speak with such clear candor and connection that the room fills with heartfelt luminosity.

Similarly, when you are communicating with others, you must prep your wood burning stove and stoke the logs well in advance with clear objectives to establish the right tone and expectations with your audience. If you've properly ignited the flame, your attendees will be engaged and follow your content because you have demonstrated how much you care about their time and attention. When you don't have established goals for your presentations, people leave your meetings cold and frustrated that their time has been wasted. In the end, you will have lost the opportunity to spark momentum for your technical work and it won't have as much lasting impact.

Hot Meetings

Many technical speakers suffer from tunnel vision when presenting. They focus too much on the granular code-level problem of the day, which prevents them from keeping in view the bigger picture goals of the overall projects and their future progress. The pressing code-level issues are important, which is why they're typically incentivized, but they are only relevant to the presentation if they line up with the specific objectives appropriate to their audiences.

When you carefully consider and define your objectives, you become more efficient and effective when presenting to your audience. Often the best approach to an effective presentation involves deciding what *not* to share, rather than what to include.

Earlier in this chapter, I referenced Elon Musk, an intense genius when it comes to ensuring that the right topics are discussed at every meeting and presentation. In his businesses, there is a clearcut separation between big picture strategic discussions and impromptu meeting assemblages intended to put out raging fires. To separate and address the latter, Musk and his teams regularly conduct spontaneous meetings known as *surges*—sometimes at midnight or in the early morning hours—to problem-solve hot issues efficiently and avoid wasting billions of dollars on failed cars, rockets, satellites, etc. Everyone in the organization knows which fire chief is on all in each department to monitor fires that might break out at any time and then work to douse them before they can spread and cause irreparable damage. Musk has created a culture in which employees are prepared to handle the worst situations with laser precision. Whether you appreciate Musk's ambitious personality or not, it's hard to disagree with the results of his unmatched output. As presenters, we can take a cue from his playbook by hyper focusing on objectives for every meeting and being intensely purposeful in every engagement, whether you're putting out fires or presenting strategies to avoid them.

Another inspiring hyper-scaler that prioritizes purposeful communication is Meta, which happens to be one of my favorite clients. I'm thankful for the opportunity to have coached hundreds of their brilliant and dedicated technical leaders, especially Francois Richard, a remarkable champion of technical storytelling. I've found that professionals such as Richard are unbelievably kind and receptive to our work. Although they face technical challenges on a planetary scale, they are willing to drop everything to focus their sole attention on coaching sessions with my team and me.

Specifically, I've always enjoyed partnering with the Meta's reliability team, which delivers top-notch resilience within a blameless and humble culture. They're so modest and supportive of the industry that they openly shared their learnings from one of the biggest tech outages in history, which took place in October 2021. Check out a talk that I helped craft with Meta's Global Head of Infrastructure, Santosh Janardhan, on the the conference website at atscaleconference.com. This event happened to have taken place during the COVID-19 pandemic, which was a peak time for social media traffic. Meta's family of apps—Facebook, Instagram, WhatsApp, and Messenger—were down for six hours, impacting billions of global users. Their mitigation and recovery mechanisms were pushed right to the edge, especially since their internal tools were also down and they were literally locked out of their own buildings. One of the keys to their efficient recovery was their ability to strategize and execute around their objectives with deliberate communications. They identified and addressed the smaller flames with targeted solutions as they progressively put out the overall fire with masterful precision. Their united commitment and effective communication not only brought their backend systems back online in record time (for this type of situation), but they also hit their goals of restoring connection for half of the world's population who rely on Meta to stay connected.

Whether we are referring to Musk's companies or Meta, we can learn from luminary-level leaders about the importance of prioritizing problems and remaining ruthlessly focused on solving them. This is especially true when collaborating with others because our communication effectiveness will make or break us, depending on how well we orient around objectives.

Keep the Main Thing as *the Main Thing*

In February 2024, when I first started writing this chapter, I experienced one of the most precious days of my life. That week, I had a particularly special daddy-daughter day on the slopes of Kirkwood Ski Resort near Lake Tahoe, CA. While driving through the frosted Sierras, I imagined heading down the slopes with my three-year-old girl. I started to get carried away as I thought about all the exciting things I was going to say and teach her. Thankfully, I was snapped out of these thoughts by the sound of my daughter kicking in her car seat and singing Christmas carols. A few things immediately struck me. First, I realized that it was early in her skiing career, and she had a long way to go before becoming Lindsey Vonn (the pro skier). Second, while I wanted to provide quality daddy-daughter time, this wasn't nearly as important as providing her with a *memorable experience*. My main priority was for her to *have fun*, so she would be more likely to spend more time with me in the future and, hopefully, take up her own interest in skiing.

I exhaled a sigh of relief, as I had barely averted making a major mistake. If I had inundated my daughter with all the amazing ins and outs of skiing, the experience might have overwhelmed, confused, and/or turned her off to the sport. She likely wouldn't have wanted to go skiing ever again because she needed to have her own unique experience and make discoveries without overwhelming outside pressure. I arrived at the conclusion that, if she didn't *have fun*, none of the other takeaways would stick. I wanted her to be free to explore her own passion at her own pace.

With this revelation in mind while on the slopes, I provided enough guidance to build her confidence and offer a few teachable moments. To avoid overdoing it, we sat down and had a brownie break. During her sugar high, I answered thirty-two questions, including why a dog was playing in the snow and identifying my favorite Christmas carol. It was around the fourteenth question that I started to become antsy. I felt as if I was wasting precious time, during which my daughter could have been taught more skiing. I was tempted to do a few more laps with her and fill her ear with expert guidance and tips…until I remembered her kicking feet and my reflection in the car. I reminded myself about the underlying objective for the day: *Facilitate fun for an overall positive experience.* Instead of pushing her limits, we finished early with a perfect run that was full of warm sun and high fives. We sang "I'm a Little Tea Pot" together to work on balance, after which she had more chocolate. When we left the slopes, her tummy was full of sweets, and my heart was filled with gratitude. I knew I'd earned many more future opportunities for quality time with her on the slopes because I stuck to my main thing.

All too often, when we plan to share an update with key stakeholders, we fall into the trap of trying to squeeze every possible detail into our slides and demos. We miss a key step in preparation: taking the time to reflect on what is essential for success and will most effectively showcase our work.

As I shared in the Introduction, my objective with this book is to enable brilliant technical leaders like you to learn the art and science of storytelling and become luminaries. To achieve my objectives, I must ensure that every word contributes to my mission and every sentence informs and/or inspires your communication competence and confidence. Hopefully, my content aligns with this objective. This rigorous adherence to my *why* prevents me from geeking out and providing too much content that would detract from my core messages (as my wife is all too familiar with when I start talking about work around the fire).

Many speakers fail because they may miss one obvious but fundamental rule of public speaking: Keep the main thing as *the main thing*. Your content might be right on target ninety percent of the time but, if the other ten percent is filled with rabbit holes and distractions, your audience might chase the distracting rabbits and your objectives might get lost in the overwhelming maze you created.

I can guess what you are thinking as you read this: Setting objectives for your technical communications and sticking to them can feel limiting because you have so many things to share that won't receive exposure. These are pressing on your mind because they are either current fires or niche areas that you are passionate about. The problem remains, if these areas aren't front of mind for your audience and relevant to your main objectives, attendees will sense you lack of focus.

The main takeaway: Focusing on objectives for your presentations sets up future success. Generating targeted content will keep your goals in sight, as well as your messaging on point. When messages are fit for the current task at hand, we engage our audience in a way that will garner support for other opportunities down the road because our audience will feel that we used their time wisely. Inversely, if we allow irrelevant clutter to distract from our current objectives, we will overwhelm our audience. Sometimes *less is a lot more*.

Intriguing Invitations

According to James Cheo, Chief Investment Officer at HSBC, professionals spend an average of 1.03 hours per day preparing slides. Over the course of a year, that's 261 hours. Who has that kind of extra time to waste? There's a better way. If you take the time to define clear goals for your communication opportunities, you can be more scrupulous about what to include and what to cut.

Here's a closing challenge: Move twenty percent of your slides to an appendix. This consolidation of your core content will force you to focus your messaging in a more effective way and give yourself about fifty-two hours—an extra hour per week—back to your calendar. Imagine how much better your actual work will be when you don't spend as much time preparing to communicate it.

Hopefully, this chapter was time well spent for you and I achieved my objective: to help you avoid one of the most common presentation pitfalls. You don't want to be the guy or gal who is known for wasting people's time. Aim to be the one who sends out meeting invites that excite your stakeholders when they accept, and later when they attend, because you have a reputation for productive discussions.

Become an effective communicator by leveraging the power of *purposeful pursuit*. If you take away just one thing from this chapter, it's that you remember to maintain *intense intentionality* as you develop content, so you can carefully craft and adapt it in a way that will pay major dividends for your career. Time is precious. Close the gap on your dream job by organizing around specific objectives and watch the recognition of your work soar.

In the next chapter, we'll take a step back to consider your overall career goals. Then you'll learn how to focus on short-term objectives with your daily communications to effectively build career progress which, ultimately, will lead toward more luminous work in the long-term.

Takeaways

- Don't waste your time creating a slapdash presentation slide deck that lacks purpose.

- Establish clear objectives to set the right tone and expectations with your audience.

- Try to focus on what *not* to share in your presentation (such as by moving twenty percent to the appendix), rather than what to nclude.

- Stick to your objectives throughout your presentations and avoid falling down rabbit holes.

- Maintain *intense intentionality* in your presentations to avoid potentially wasting your attendees' precious time.

CHAPTER FOUR

Orient Around Objectives—Part Two

On November 18, 2011, a close nineteen-year-old family friend named Joshua "Chachi" Corral was stationed in Afghanistan during his military service. While sweeping for mines in front of his fellow troops, one exploded and took his life. The loss was devastating, as Chachi was like a brother to me. Since that tragic event, I have come to regard him as something of a warrior angel. He continues to inspire me and everyone else who knew him. Chachi's passing lit a new fire in my soul, which was monumental during the formation of Light Up Ventures. Today, the flame burns stronger than ever.

I share this as a reminder of how precious life is and to emphasize that we need to make the most of each day. The average American employee spends 90,000 hours of her or his life at work, which is a clear signal that we ought to find ways to *purposefully pursue* what we do with a maximum amount of passion and intentionality.

Like many other people, there was a time when I was sucked into the daily grind of showing up, checking boxes, and clocking out. This included how I approached my meetings and communication with others. Inspired by Chachi's memory, I have since made my life more *intentional* and try to make interactions more *meaningful*.

Take a moment to close your eyes and visualize your future as you near retirement age. After having spent approximately 4,000 days of your lifetime working, you likely have built quite an impressive resume. Still, do you think you could have left behind a greater legacy of accomplishment and impact if you had shown up with more purpose?

During my executive coaching sessions with senior leaders, we focus on establishing near and long-term goals to ensure they live out each day with focused intention. Whether they are crafting organizational charts for increased productivity or carving out margins in their calendar for more time with their families, being deliberate infuses everything we do with greater meaning.

Now that we're about one-third through our developmental journey together, I'm going to challenge you to dig deeper. I don't want you or your audiences to miss out on all that you have to offer because your communications weren't as impactful as possible. Here is the billion-dollar question for you to answer: *Why do you work?*

Start with the End

One of the most influential books of all time is Stephen Covey's *The 7 Habits of Highly Successful People*. According to the publisher, it's sold over twenty-five million copies in thirty-eight languages. The book contains many best practices that have changed my life, but one has stuck with me to this day: "Start with the end in mind."

Let's channel Covey's philosophy as you look to orient your daily communications. Ask yourself the following: *What do I want to achieve down the road? Where do I hope to be in my career—two, ten, and twenty years from now? How do I fill my work hours with meaning? What do I want to do with my time? Which individuals would I choose to work with if I were to have a choice?*

As you start shoveling beneath the surface, don't worry about carving out perfect holes. Many of your reflections will turn to dust that flies away with the wind of life's circumstances. Reflecting is a means, not an end. Frequently asking yourself what is important to you now—as well as in the future—opens windows into possibilities to motivate you to perform daily tasks with more direction and purpose. I liken this to planning a trip utilizing Google Maps: You have a specific destination in mind but can add stops along the way that serve as catalytic checkpoints.

In addition to the reflective questions that I posed above, here are three more practical tips for analyzing and enabling your career trajectory:

1. Read *The 7 Habits of Highly Successful People*—as well as a few other titles in the Suggested Readings (page 193) in the back of the book—to adopt additional guidance for career progress.

2. Surround yourself with wise counsel—coaches, mentors, or trusted confidants—who can support your planning with wisdom, honesty, and encouragement. Invite others into your circle, especially individuals who have blazed trails that inspire you.

3. Take the time to slow down and find solitude. When I coach ambitious clients, I encourage them to do something that at first seems impossible: *Sit still.* Connecting to your inner self without moving or speaking helps surface more clarity and peace, so you can leverage refreshing energy as you lean into what's next.

What's Your Destination?

Let's return to the Google Maps analogy. Say you decide that your ultimate destination is to become CTO (Chief Technology Officer) of a mid-sized tech company. You would identify key career stops you must make along the way that provide you with the experience and opportunities you'll need to ultimately make it to that level. If you're currently a senior software engineer, you might work with your manager to create a roadmap that itemizes the benchmarks you need to get to each progressively higher job title:

- People management skills to become an engineering manager.

- Strategic planning experience to become a director.

- Corporate financial competence to become a VP.

- A board of directors role to prepare you for executive responsibilities.

Once you've gained the knowledge and experience to build your resume with several measurable accomplishments, you will be ready to arrive at your ultimate destination: the CTO title.

My late friend Chachi, whom I mentioned at the beginning of the chapter, knew from a young age that he wanted *to be a light* for the people around him. In fact, those were some of his last words to his closest comrades and family before he died in Afghanistan. His long-term goal was to become a shining beacon for others by demonstrating faith and love. To accomplish this, he placed military service as the first stop on his journey, as it enabled him to serve his fellow troops and his country. In the end, his dedicated sacrifice led to surpassing his goals in ways he couldn't have imagined when he first set them.

Presentation Precision

As discussed in the previous chapter, whether it's state-of-the-art cars or innovative rockets, Elon Musk is a disruptor. But he doesn't do this just to shake things up; he constantly experiments and tests against the status quo because he knows there are always opportunities for optimization that lead to breakthrough innovation.

It doesn't matter if you're like Musk and enjoy solving hard user problems, or if you prefer to hang out behind the scenes for backend development. Either way, you ought to be creative in your approach to presentations if you want to increase the impact of your work. You need to disrupt the status quo of how you've thought about effective communication.

Your everyday communications are the threads that connect you from one stop to the next in your short- and long-term career efforts. Your presentations will succeed if you create objectives and build content around them. Your audience members will become your biggest career champions, simply based on their experiences having heard you speak about your work.

Now that you have a better understanding of your broader career goals and the importance of communication skills to achieve them, let's zoom in on the objectives for your day-to-day presentations with best practices that will ensure ultimate effectiveness.

Like our approach to analyzing your audience established in Chapter Two, let's start with a simple question. This will help you line up your presentation preparation for maximum effectiveness, just as Luke did when he shot a perfectly aimed missile into the core of the Death Star.

Why Are You Speaking?

I realize the above might seem like an overly simplified question, so permit me to help by listing a few sample objectives from technical leaders who have presented to various audiences:

Adopt system	Inspire trust
Decide direction	Grow confidence
Solicit feedback	Convey excitement
Confirm alignment	Build rapport
Create plan	Mend relationships

I left the top two cells in both columns blank for a reason: They represent the categories to fill in for potential presentation objectives. Before I reveal the correct categories look over each example objective and try to figure out how they're distinguished. Do you have any guesses in terms of what the categories might be?

When we review this exercise during training sessions, participants offer a variety of responses. They almost always overthink the dichotomy of the two categories. The information you present is often complicated enough, so let's keep the objectives of your presentations simple to increase your chances of achieving them. The two categories are—drum roll please—"do" (left table column) and "feel" (right table column).

After an audience hears your presentation, are you looking for attendees to take any specific action—in other words, *do* something? Or are you hoping to elicit an emotional response—that is, *feel* something?

The simple beauty of this approach is that the two categories aren't mutually exclusive. For example, what happens when the decision maker gives actionable approval for a group to *do* a large technical project? Everyone involved *feels* excited to work on it!

Pillars of Persuasion

A balance of *logical* appeal and *emotional* resonance delivered with *credibility* can help guide your presentation objectives. As we briefly discussed in Chapter Two, Aristotle's pillars of persuasion—*ethos, logos,* and *pathos*—may also be helpful for organizing your objectives. I like to simplify these concepts in our training curriculum by rephrasing them with some alliteration: credibility (*ethos*); clarity (*logos*); and conviction (*pathos*).

When you're deciding upon your desired outcomes for a communication opportunity, consider what you want your audience to be thinking and feeling while hearing you speak. Do you want them to see you as a credible thought leader who can be trusted with the strategy and execution of a technical project (*ethos*)? Or has there been some confusion about roles and responsibilities regarding the development and deployment of a new data system, so you hope to present a logical update that enables everyone to clearly understand her or his involvement (*logos*)? Or maybe morale on your team is low because senior management keeps changing their minds about infrastructure investments, so you want to instill some motivating grit in your team that will help them become optimistic about the roadmap (*pathos*)?

If you're a technical leader, you've probably already experienced a version of each of these scenarios, so below are a few practical tips for orienting objectives around each pillar:

Credibility *(ethos)*
- When seeking to earn the respect of stakeholders, leverage the Harvard Business Research mentioned in the Introduction about first impressions by conveying *trust* and *competence*.

- Demonstrate trust and competence by modestly mentioning how your past experiences equipped you with relevant expertise for the current project.

- Back up your anecdotal experience with objective support by sharing the measurable impact you've made in similar situations.

- Name drop a handful of prominent projects, achievements, partners, or customers that can boost your audience's perception about your trustworthiness as a thought leader; however, be careful not to go overboard at the risk of coming across as arrogant.

- Share how you solved similar complex problems in the past to demonstrate your credibility for solving the ones you are about to discuss.

Clarity *(logos)*
- When addressing confusion and aiming for clear communication, conduct root-cause analysis, so you can tackle the core underlying problems with precise comments.

- As discussed in Part One, Empathetic Effectiveness, remember that message clarity comes from a proper understanding of your attendees and their familiarity with your work.

- Avoid overly technical jargon, unknown acronyms, and weedy deep dives. Otherwise, your audience might lose interest and/or won't be able to understand and retain your main messages.

- If colleagues have been struggling to understand the status of a particular project, you can improve awareness by sending or posting regular status updates in which you will inform them of the exact timing with measurable milestones and metrics to evaluate progress.

- If there has been confusion about the problem space for a particular technical project, present the various issues in the form of questions that you can answer succinctly.

Conviction *(pathos)*
- Technical presenters often overlook the emotional aspects of communication because they are typically linear thinkers focused on rational problem solving. Sometimes it's helpful to find out how audience members feel about a particular discussion and demonstrate empathy to show that you understand and relate to them.

- Acknowledge the technical pain points—i.e., latency, tech debt, bugs, outages, etc.—your audience experiences and then sympathetically demonstrate your awareness of their concerns by addressing them directly during your presentation.

- Offer examples of how you experienced and solved for similar pain points in the past to earn the audiences' trust.

- Avoid describing situations with rose-colored glasses and overly optimistic perspectives that might mislead your audience and diminish your credibility. If a project has challenges, it's better to be transparent about them—including mentioning failures—and bring them out in the open in a balanced tone. (Don't go overboard: The sky is never *actually* falling.) If you wish to boost morale during such circumstances, remind them about the project's goals and upsides and offer potential ways in which the problems may be converted to opportunities.

- If your goal is to convince people of your solutions to technical problems, make sure to craft talking points and deliver them in a way that conveys your conviction, as the right amount of confidence can be contagious. (We'll cover more on delivery techniques in Chapter Eight.)

Asynchronous Alignment

Let's pretend we're hopping back on board the Golden Gate ferry, which we rode in Chapter One. Prior to the trip, we'd heard some interesting things about the historic sites around the San Francisco Bay and even seen photographs of them, but now we're looking forward to experiencing them for ourselves. The trip brochure provided a brief overview of what to expect on the boat ride, including the magnificent architecture of the Golden Gate Bridge, spooky stories about Alcatraz, and some unique history about the people who shaped the region. As we take our seats, Fran takes the place of the architect who scared us on our last ride. She introduces herself as our tour guide while we review the brochure materials about what to expect on our journey with her.

As presenters, it's helpful to set our audience's expectations as early as possible to increase the chances of us achieving our objectives. In many cases, this can be done in advance of a presentation. For example, a few brief bullets may be added to the meeting invite or to a status tracker. Sometimes it can be helpful to post an abstract on the topic ahead of time on an event website, the company's Intranet, or a shared Slack channel. By setting expectations and engaging with invitees in advance, you are putting the audience at ease because they feel a sense of control and can plan to engage accordingly, since they have an idea of what's coming, as well as see that you're prepared to make good use of their time. When your audience is primed, you can orient and align their experience around your objectives and perhaps even energize them.

Meanwhile, back on the boat we settle in with Irish coffee, inhale the salty sea breeze, and bask in the California sun as Fran delivers her opening spiel. She starts out by immediately teasing that on our way back from Alcatraz we'll finish the tour with some eerie ghost stories about Al Capone on our way back from Alcatraz, which causes us to perk up with excitement. After the brief teaser to immediately hook our attention, Fran switches gears to share how she had grown up in San Francisco and therefore has a personal connection to the city and the sites to come. She rattles off highlights of her background, including how many tours she's led, her official docent certifications from having served as a Bay area museum guide, and her native San Franciscan roots. Then she pauses her commentary, so we can immerse ourselves in the special sounds of the Bay and collect our thoughts.

Fran has excelled at achieving her first objectives: earning our attention and establishing credibility, so we can trust her for the rest of her tour. By contrast, when many developers begin their presentations, they forget to make personal introductions. This simple omission causes them to miss an opportunity to engage their audience right from the start. In Chapter Six, I'll share more about how to introduce yourself in a natural way that warms up attendees and establishes your credibility without any hint of narcissism.

As the boat heads toward the famous Golden Gate Bridge, Fran starts her storytelling with some historical context to draw us in before smoothly transitioning to an overview of the structure's architectural highlights with a deep dive about some technical innovations. She gradually builds up her narrative, emphasizing the need for ongoing bridge maintenance to keep the site beautiful and functioning. At the end of the discussion, she offers a clear call to action (CTA): asking for donations to sustain the bridge. Nearly everyone on the tour chips in with some venmo payments, mainly because of the resounding clarity of her storytelling.

Next, we arrive at the spot we've all been waiting for: Alcatraz Island. The boat slows down as we approach the big rock with flocking seagulls and gray clouds sneaking in overhead. Fran lowers her voice to an intriguing tone that aligns with the compelling content she's about to share. We lean in as she tells the story of Alcatraz inmate and notorious gangster Al Capone, whose nasty crimes have become legendary. She proceeds to describe his incarceration at the heavily guarded prison, ending the tale with his death and how his banjo-playing apparition has been spotted in the shower block. She subtly transitions to an intense story of an attempted prison escape, causing our eyes to widen until she suddenly shouts, "*Bang*! The poor, cold prisoner was shot down while running in the dark toward the freezing water." She pauses, allowing the vivid image to sink in.

What had Fran done so effectively? She had teased about the Capone ghost story in the beginning and then later delivered the goods. She brought the group's attention back to the introduction using what is known as a "looping" technique, which we'll cover further in Chapter Six. As icing on the cake, she added the bonus of an exhilarating story about a frightening prison escape.

The emotional aspects of technical presentations are often shrugged off as unnecessary fluff. While I agree that too much drama or hype can cross over the line to making one sound like a car salesman, we must not forget that all attendees—whether they are technical professionals or not—have human wiring and search for emotional connections, whether they recognize them or not. As a speaker, you must learn how to build and utilize all three pillars (credibility, clarity, and conviction) to support your audience's attention.

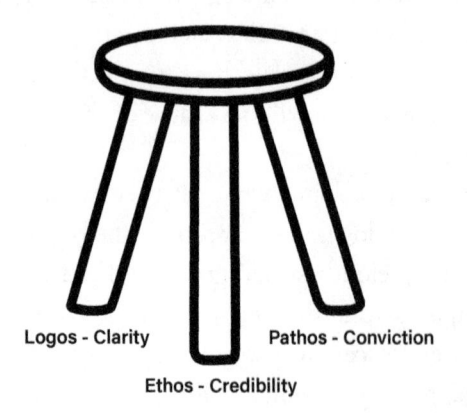

Logos - Clarity **Pathos - Conviction**
Ethos - Credibility

When we leverage the power of Aristotle's pillars of persuasion, we construct a three-legged stool for engaging communication that maximizes effectiveness through ethos, logos, and pathos, ultimately enabling us to achieve our objectives. Fran connected with credibility in her introduction; logically presented her messages to establish clarity; and won everyone over with emotional appeal that sealed the deal with conviction. Her superlative skills as a tour guide ensured that her information would remain with us and that we would recommend her services to others in the future.

Burn Bright

In the last chapter, I mentioned the joy I receive from deep conversations I have with my wife by a fire. While we sip our coffee, we receive two benefits from the fire: warmth and light. This is especially the case on cold winter evenings when the sun sets early. The flame brightens the room with a luminosity that helps us see each other in a special way during our conversations. At the same time, the fire provides our bodies and souls with nourishing warmth.

During your presentations, your goal is to fill the room with light and warmth. The light shines in the form of brilliant, easy-to-follow explanations that inform the audience and illuminate your technical work and its impact. The warmth is emitted through an intentional tone with inspiring messages that heat up excitement about your efforts.

SIDECAR

Clear articulation delivers your audience from the *darkness of confusion* into the *light of comprehension.*

A dry, emotionless presentation will fall on deaf ears. While you must convey certain facts and share rational perspectives, it's equally as important to balance your logical messaging with credible background about yourself to demonstrate you are human and authentically relate to the challenges your audience faces. It's okay to open yourself up a bit and share your warmth—even when you are discussing a technical subject. In addition to your relevant background, you can further the emotional appeal throughout your presentations by infusing intriguing details about your technical work in a way that compels your audience to support your ambitious endeavors.

To summarize, always remember the two most important objectives for technical communications: *inform* (educate people so they can *think* clearly) and *inspire* (influence people so they can act enthusiastically). Depending on your audience and the subject matter, you may add some weight to one side or the other, but there should always be a healthy balance of both. No matter how much an engineer claims he or she "just wants the facts," your delivery method must always include a certain level of inspiration to trigger emotions that increase engagement.

Practical Closing Tips

I'm now going to provide you with three practical tips that will help your presentations become perceived as time well spent by all concerned, because nobody enjoys wasting an hour listening to a boring presentation that didn't seem to have any point.

Practical Tip #1: *Adjust Your Aim*

If you're near a whiteboard when preparing your presentation, draw a target with three circles like the one on the following page. (If a whiteboard is unavailable, you can use a sticky note.) The three circles represent the typical audience sizes for your technical presentations. The outermost circle represents large group opportunities (i.e., tech conferences, All Hands, etc.), the middle circle represents small group settings (i.e., department gatherings, team meetings, etc.), and the inner circle represents 1:1 conversations (i.e., manager meetings, partner check-ins, etc.).

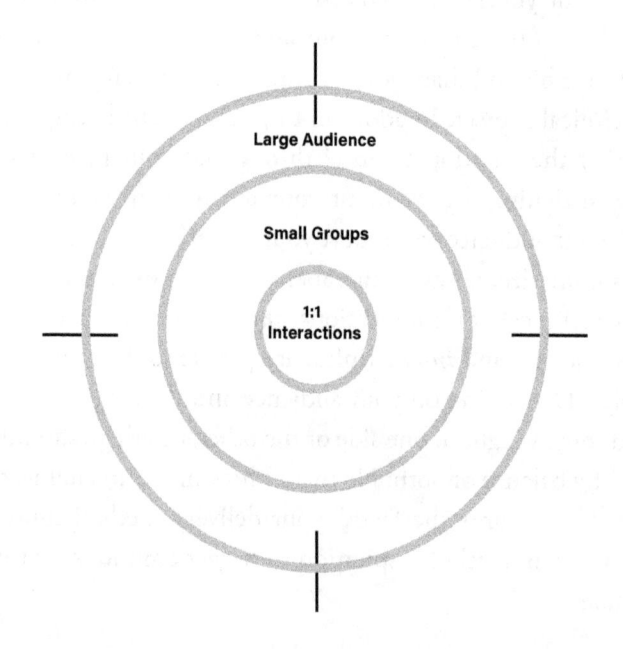

Large Audience

Small Groups

1:1 Interactions

While you are defining objectives for your presentations, consider the size of your audience, so that you can shape your talking points accordingly. Larger groups are likely going to have a more heterogeneous population with a broader diversity of attendees and varying levels of familiarity with—and interest in—your work. When you present to them, you should aim your messaging to broadly cover the edges of the scope of your work, thereby maximizing the chances of engaging them.

When it comes to communicating to the inner circles, you will want to curate your messaging with more personal specificity. You will have a better sense of the wants, needs, and perspectives of a smaller group or individual, which means you can curate the details you know will be of value without overwhelming them with stuff they already know or have no interest in hearing.

Practical Tip #2: *Less Is More*

My love of working with heat sometimes gets me in trouble. I'm introverted, so when my wife and I host people at our house, I prefer to hide in the kitchen behind the stove while I cook meals. My perfectionism causes me to overly focus on landing every dish at the exact same time, which also causes me to overstuff the stove, so I don't have to worry about it while I'm cooking. And because I'm so caught up in cooking, I fail to realize that the raging fireplace has raised the temperature of the house too fast. The result is an unintentionally overheated house and sweaty, uncomfortable guests.

Similarly, technical leaders tend to cram too much information into their presentations. To avoid making your audience break out into a sweat from technical overload, remember that there are two types of presentations: the "delivered" version that you vocalize to your audience, and the "handout" version, which includes the deck and your notes in much greater detail that they can review at their leisure. Keeping your verbal presentation succinct means that your presentation will be tight and focused, and your audience will feel comfortable with the appropriate amount of content. At the same time, the handouts ensure that they won't miss anything and can absorb however much they like at their own pace.

Practical Tip #3: Fewer Slides
The third and final practical tip is also tied to proper precision. You want to avoid flooding attendees with unnecessary clutter and chaos on the screen. The text on your slides should be minimalist since you will be speaking to these points anyway. Additionally, consider reducing the total number of slides that you share.

Go at a consistent, steady pace and be sure to take a breath or a drink of water every now and then. You'll find that your audience tracks with you and appreciates your methodical approach.

How many times have you attended presentations in which the speaker went through dozens of slides, realized she was running out of time, and then had to race through the final pages at the expense of time for discussion? The simple way to avoid this situation is to err on the side of cutting out as many slides as possible. If a final deck for

---

SIDECAR

Slow it down! There is a tendency for nervous or passionate speakers to hurry up and speed through their presentations, which detracts from their effectiveness. This tends to have the opposite effect in terms of presentation quality. The more rushed you are, the greater chance you will lose your place and fumble with words. Worse, there is a good chance that some people in your audience won't be able to keep up with you, so they tune out. Go at a consistent, steady pace and be sure to take a breath or a drink of water every now and then. You'll find that your audience tracks with you and appreciates your methodical approach.

a twenty-minute talk has twenty-four slides, for example, condense or delete them until you are down to eighteen to twenty (spending no more than one minute per slide). At first, you'll probably be resistant and feel that everything is critical; if you edit something out, it will come across as a glaring omission. Guess what? No one will ever notice the difference. The upside is that you can then present your content at a comfortable pace without hurrying things along at the end or skipping crucial pieces. If you're worried that less content will inhibit your audience's understanding, you can always include that supplemental content in the handout version of your deck.

Trust me on this: Your audience will be far more appreciative of a tight presentation with fewer slides than a lengthy one that rambles on too long (more to come about slide design in Chapter Eight). This is why I will now fight the temptation to expand my guidance on objectives in this chapter and finish succinctly with some key takeaways.

Takeaways

- Recognize that life is precious, which means you need to make the most out of each day.

- Determine your career destination and then figure out what steps you need to take to get there with intentional communication along the way.

- The pillars of persuasion—credibility (*ethos*), clarity (*logos*), and conviction (*pathos*)—can help you organize and achieve your objectives.

- Simplify your objectives by orienting around the two key categories of effective presentations: What do you want your audience to "do" and/or "feel"?

- Limit the amount of content on each slide and edit down your total number of slides as much as possible.

- Always remember the two most important objectives for technical communications: *inform* (help people think) and *inspire* (help people act).

ACT II

*Story*telling—The *What*

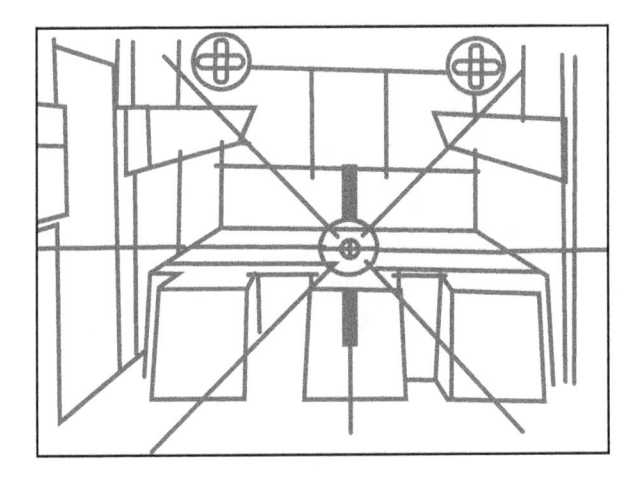

CHAPTER FIVE

Craft Content—Part One

As mentioned in previous chapters, the left side of our brain is responsible for linear thinking; it processes information more efficiently when the inputs are organized logically. If the neural pathways are clear, we are at an optimal level of being able to accurately interpret the signals and act upon them. By contrast, if our brains are overcluttered, the information is perceived as random, and it becomes difficult for us to understand and act upon.

Empathetic effectiveness serves as a filter for the next two parts of our communication framework. Like a funnel with a grate, we can screen our messages through our understanding of our audience (ensure empathy) and why we're speaking to them (enable effectiveness). Proper audience analysis and stated objectives help determine which pieces of information should be poured into the funnel and be permitted to filter through the screen and into our presentations. The unnecessary bits are trapped by the filter and omitted from the presentation, creating a tight deck that is fully tuned in to the needs of the audience without leaving any room for distraction.

Once our messages pass through the above system and resonate with our audience, we can move to next phase of growing our luminosity, which happens to be my personal favorite: *storytelling*.

Like software code, stories add meaning and functionality to words. They organize information in a way that is easier for our audience to process, understand, and act upon while also offering emotional, relatable checkpoints that engage everyone's attention. By crafting words in a functional manner, the messages become colorful and stand out better than black and white facts.

The technical problems that you experience every day at work are complicated enough. Your goal is to produce content that explains your work in simple terms, so it has the best chance of being understood and embraced with your action items enthusiastically set into motion.

When it comes to the royal palace of communications, the adage "content is king" poorly allocates authority within the communication ecosystem. Instead, we should treat the *recipients* of our presentations as royalty, providing these queens and kings with entertaining, informative and inspiring messages.

Dr. Martin Luther King, Jr., widely regarded as one of the greatest orators of our time, told stories that *turned moments into movements*. His famous words "I have a dream" certainly left an indelible mark, but it was his scintillating storytelling and deep passion that mesmerized his listeners and transformed them into becoming advocates of his messages.

East Meets West

Li Zheng, Global Head of Product Data Science at Genentech, grew up in China before moving to the United States, where she earned a Masters in Biostatistics from the University of Massachusetts, as well as an MBA from Northeastern University. Her educational pedigree is second to none, but what's even more impressive is her ability to communicate her technical pharmaceutical work in such a way that she impacts millions of medical patients around the globe.

Over the years, Li has led a variety of biotech teams, which has given her a platform from which she can demonstrate her unique ability to connect the dots of highly complex technical opportunities. Her superpower doesn't end there. Once she has connected the dots, she communicates the bigger picture to stakeholders, who often have varying levels of familiarity with her teams' work. She delivers her messaging with such a personal touch that audiences can process the information and act upon it.

It's not an easy task to explain data science details to people who have a wide range of expertise on the subject. Biotechnical work—especially cutting-edge drug development—also involves intense collaboration across various departments. Ideas and data points often transition from lab technicians to data scientists, from systems administrators to pre-clinical trials, from final institutional approvals before products are distributed to the end users (patients in need).

Li's ability to communicate effectively inside and outside her company make her a quintessential luminary. What inspires me most, however, is that she has reached such heights of accomplishment even though interpersonal communication was initially challenging for her, given her lingual and cultural learning curves. When she moved from China to the United States, she adapted her communication style and fully embraced the power of storytelling to inform and influence some of the brightest minds on the planet. She can address upper echelon board members, brilliant scientists, and aspiring college graduates with equal eloquence.

It's been a privilege to know Li for over the years and help her gift for storytelling blossom. I'll share the key secrets of effective storytelling concepts that I offer Li and my other luminary clients in the pages that follow.

More What

In the next chapter, I will provide you with three story frameworks that will serve as flexible templates for you to plug and play your technical work in a more organized fashion to better engage your audiences. To properly build the foundation for those frameworks, I will explain what stories are and why they're important.

As I've been modeling throughout this book, stories help guide our audiences from one subject and/or point to another. This technique, known as *sign posting*, helps audiences follow where you have taken them and anticipate where they are going with you.

Personally, I don't find Webster's definition of the word *story* all that useful: "(a) an account of incidents or events; (b) a statement regarding the facts pertinent to a situation in question." What's more helpful is the etymology of the word dating to ancient Latin: *historia*.

Since *historia* is also the original form of *history*, I believe it's a better way of framing the word for our purposes. We can say that a luminary's content reflects "her/his story" of their respective work.

Simply stated, a story is an account of your work. It's the *who, what, why, how,* and lastly *when* (which is often overlooked but a highly important element in technical presentations) bound together by a central purpose and underlying context that appeals on both logical and emotional levels. A good story organizes information about your technical work in a way that is easy for an audience to follow and potentially act on.

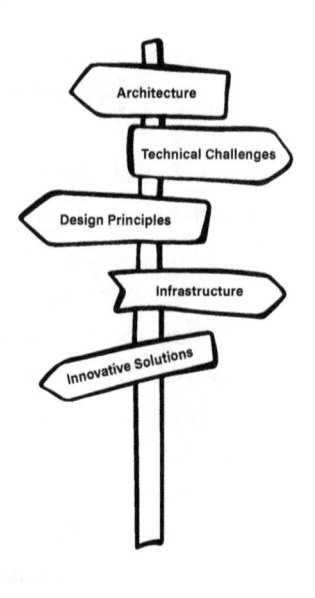

Our brains are hardwired to receive information in the form of story. One of my favorite quotes is from legendary filmmaker Alfred

Hitchcock, who describes *drama*—which may be substituted by the word *story*—as "life with the dull parts taken out." Great stories cut to the chase and can answer the following questions from listeners:

- *What happened?*
- *When did it happen?*
- *Why did that take place?*
- *Who was involved?*
- *How did it occur?*
- *What's going to happen next?*

Throughout history—from cave drawings representing battles to contemporary speeches that have influenced the fate of nations—stories connect the communicators to the listeners or viewers. They serve as bridges that allow you to assemble, wrap, carry, and deliver a version of a tale from your unique perspective to others.

A compelling story is crucial to any successful presentation. When a speaker fails to deliver this, the result is a random grab-bag of information that causes a wide disconnect between her and the audience.

More Why

According to behavioral scientist and speaker Jennifer Aaker, "Stories are remembered up to twenty-two times more than facts alone." To illustrate this point, let's return to our SRE friend Relli and his data center tour.

In the beginning, Relli lacked empathetic effectiveness, selfishly sprinting through his presentation and causing his audience to be left in the dark. From the cold start in the lobby to his overwhelming technical explanations, his information dump fell flat—especially among the less technical visitors. Why was his performance such a failure? Because he didn't turn his information into crafted content or transform the disconnected data into an insightful story.

Let's suppose Relli receives constructive feedback after his tour and takes it to heart, working on improving his presentation skills. He starts off his next tour by asking questions upfront to analyze his visitors and identify their expectations. He establishes objectives and sticks to them throughout the tour. Along the way, Relli shares his data center work in the form of a story, which engages the audience, connects to their needs, and helps illustrate his objectives.

Relli's improved introductory comments might look more like this:

> *Hello, thanks for coming to our state-of-the-art data center. I know your time is valuable, so we'll get right to it with a fun quick fact: The lobby you're standing in is 300 square feet out of a total 100 thousand square feet that powers the traffic of our most important user apps.*
>
> *We're proud to host groups from all around the world who are often users of our apps. I know that your group includes a diverse mix of DC engineers like myself, as well as product and business leaders, so I plan to start by sharing some broader context about the data center before walking you through some technical innovations. I'll close by detailing the outstanding impact of the center.*
>
> *As you can see, I'm passionate about DC operations and prefer to make these tours as interactive as possible, so please feel free to ask questions along the way.*
>
> *Before we move on to the main part of the center's technical innovations, most visitors find it helpful to first learn what a DC is and know why it's important. The simplest way to answer these questions is by asking you to pull out your phones and flip to one of our user apps. When you or another one of our billions of users interact with our app, it processes trillions of petabytes of data with our backend software systems. Those*

backend software systems stack on top of each other like a massive technology cake that sits on top of a hardware platter. The hardware platter is made of millions of machines that are also stacked on top of each other in racks, which are housed in data centers like this one.

In partnership with teams such as yours, our work ensures that users can open apps that function properly and make them happy. Of course, our work isn't without occasional glitches. We have had our share of long nights as a result of outages that sometimes cause the apps to crash and users to be upset.

In response to these issues, we've spent the last few years focusing on three core technology solutions that have greatly reduced the number of unhappy situations for users.

I'd like to invite you to follow me into the main warehouse, where you will hear about our three innovative solutions for these problems in greater detail.

Let's itemize the things Relli did correctly this time around:

1. He gave a warm opening in which he thanked the attendees for coming, acknowledged that they are busy people, and said he would make sure their time was going to be well spent (*empathetic effectiveness*).

2. He started strong by hooking the audience's attention with some quick compelling statistics.

3. He established a strong first impression by demonstrating his competence and passion for DCs.

4. He earned the trust of his audience by acknowledging he knew who they were.

5. Since he knew his audience, he was able to set expectations and tease some interesting points to come on the tour.

6. He brought everyone on the same page by concisely explaining basic information about what a DC is and does.

7. He made the tour interactive by having visitors use their phones and engage with their apps.

8. He spelled out the bigger picture impact of the work in the DC.

9. He demonstrated empathy by admitting to technical glitches that had caused the users some pain.

10. Rather than dwelling too much on the glitches, he jumped right into the three upbeat innovative solutions as he transitioned to the next section of his tour (while walking from the lobby into the warehouse).

Relli continues to be on a roll as he leads the tour group into the main warehouse:

> *Watch your step! As you can see, we have AI robots buzzing around everywhere to help automate our processes that we've continued to optimize over the years. You can also see the neatly organized rows of machines that I mentioned earlier that make up the bottom hardware plate of our software cake. What you're hearing is our ultra-innovative, water-based cooling system with fans that keep our machines from melting.*

As I mentioned, a few years ago we had some glitches in the functionality of our apps that caused a decrease in engagement among our users. Some of those glitches came from the complexity that you're seeing around this massive warehouse.

At the end of the tour, I'll show our interactive real-time dashboards, which display fascinating trends that highlight the roller coaster we were on before we were able to stabilize all of the complex hardware that you're seeing. Before we dive into the three technical innovations that helped solve for our complexities, I'd like you to look over at that large rollup door, which is where all of our hardware shipments arrive. That door used to open once a month for new parts, but it is now constantly opened weekly to welcome in the hundreds of thousands of GPUs that continue to fill our data center with bleeding-edge AI capabilities.

With this broader context about the overall DC and some of it's exciting areas in mind, let's dive into the three technical innovations that help keep our apps running with reliable dependability.

[Here Relli would fill in the details of the three takeaways following this framework.] We resolved the overall problem of reliability by focusing on challenge 1A [details about complexity] so we could move on to the next technical problem.

This is why we developed solution 1B [details about novelty] that delivered results 1C [details about impact].

Once we finished implementing solution 1B, we then moved on to challenge 2A [details about complexity] by developing solution 2B [details about novelty] that helped delivered results 2C [details about impact].

After implementing solution 2B, we solved final challenge 3A [details about complexity] with solution 3B [details about novelty] that delivered results 3C [details about impact].

> *Now that we've walked through the three core areas of the warehouse, I'd like to show you the final stop, which I mentioned earlier. This area will blow your mind in terms of how it provides fascinating real-time user traffic insights.*

In the above, I obviously didn't include specific details about each sub-topic (challenge, solution, impact—all in brackets), but I think you'll follow the key improvements Relli made to the middle part of his tour and story:

1. He transitioned from his introduction with some illustrative context (mention of "the robots"), which provided some entertainment.

2. He re-emphasized the overarching, bigger-picture problems.

3. He methodically broke his core content into three sub-sections, so his visitors could connect actual circumstances with what they were seeing.

4. He provided three elements that are essential for technical messaging: complexity (challenges), novelty (solutions), and impact (results).

5. He built excitement leading up to the final part of the tour.

Relli now heads into the home stretch with the third part of his presentation: the closing.

I know those technical innovations can seem a bit overwhelming if you aren't an engineer, but hopefully, you were able to follow the main parts about how we're continuing to improve our back end to keep users happy on the front end.

Speaking of the front, the large monitors you're looking at show graphs with real-time insights based on actual user traffic data. In this longer-term graph on the left, you can see how we've continued to increase overall reliability since we initiated technical solution 1A.

The middle graph shows specific results from each of the three individual solutions that I just showed you back in the warehouse. Notice how they ladder up to the bigger reliability picture.

The last graph on the right shows future projections, so we can plan to sustain our operations for years to come.

I'll share one more exciting announcement about what's in the future, but first I would like to wrap up the tour by leaving you with three takeaways in case you want to share them with our colleagues back at your offices. *[Relli states the three takeaways tied to the three sub-sections he shared during the middle of his tour.]*

To officially close our tour, it's my honor to announce that we're breaking ground on our next state-of-the-art data center next week in downtown Techville. It will house hundreds of thousands of GPU chips to power cutting-edge AGI innovations and make users even happier for many years to come.

Thank you so much for joining me today. I hope this was well worth your time.

I'll now take some questions and leave you with my email in case you'd like to stay in touch.

Relli finished well in his closing comments by doing the following:

- He transitioned from the main technical section with sympathy to connect with less technical attendees.

- He pointed out visuals highlighting the measurable successes of the solutions.

- He summed up takeaways for visitors to remember and to take back to those who did not attend, potentially encouraging more engagement around his work.

- He inspired the audience by sharing an exciting surprise announcement about the new state-of-the-art DC plans.

- He closed by thanking attendees for joining him, took some questions, and then invited people to stay in touch via his contact information.

> **SIDECAR**
>
> Have you ever wondered how Netflix has become such a juggernaut in a crowded field? One key to their success is technical innovation. The streaming giant utilizes thirty-six drives that can hold approximately one hundred terabytes of data. Their servers can store 20,000 movies at the same time. The company leverages this infrastructure to analyze consumer viewer data and then provides highly personalized suggestions for shows and movies. They utilize the power of story to transform overwhelming amounts of information into binge-worthy entertainment. Even the company's vision speaks to storytelling: "At Netflix, we aspire to entertain the world–creating great stories from anywhere and offering greater choice and control for people everywhere."

By now, you should have a complete understanding of the power of good storytelling and why it's so important to help engage audiences. In the next chapter, I'll share practical tips for how to leverage proven frameworks for technical storytelling that you can use for your presentations.

Before I provide the takeaways, I would like to close with where we started and let legendary luminary Dr. Martin Luther King, Jr. conclude the chapter, as his amplified messages continue to reverberate around the world today...

> *I have a dream that one day this nation will rise up and live out the true meaning of its creed: We hold these truths to be self-evident, that all men are created equal.*

Takeaways

- Empathetic effectiveness enables more powerful content.

- Storytelling is remembered up to twenty-two times more than facts alone.

- Stories add functionality to words and organize information in a way that is easier for our audience to process, understand, and act upon.

- Presentations in the form of stories to maintain engagement with your audiences by guiding them through the milestones of your technical work (especially when they use *signposting*).

- Storytelling has the power to turn moments into movements.

CHAPTER SIX

Craft Content—Part Two

January 9th, 2007: It was on this brisk day at Moscone Center in San Francisco, CA that Steve Jobs took the stage in front of a packed audience full of developers, reporters, and other technology enthusiasts and illuminated them with top-notch storytelling. Jobs had labored hundreds of hours in preparation of this much-anticipated event, carefully selecting and refining every word and rehearsing his delivery until every talking point flowed smoothly with just the right intonation. People leaned forward at the edge of their seats as Jobs appeared in his trademark black turtleneck and began his presentation.

> *This is the day I've been looking forward to for two and a half years.*
> *Every once in a while, a revolutionary product comes along that changes everything...*
> *[In]1984, we introduced the Macintosh. It didn't just change Apple. It changed the whole computer industry.*
> *In 2001, we introduced the first iPod. And it didn't just*

change the way we all listen to music, it changed the entire music industry.

Well, today we're introducing three revolutionary products of this class. The first one is a widescreen iPod with touch controls. The second is a revolutionary mobile phone.

And the third is a breakthrough Internet communications device...

The audience was reeled in—hook, line, and sinker. Jobs created magic right in front of their eyes, tantalizing them with his unparalleled storytelling ability and converting them into evangelists for his company's products.

Fifteen years later, also in San Francisco, Li Zheng—mentioned in the previous chapter—addressed a large audience full of technical colleagues to contribute her thought leadership at an important company conference. She shared messages that illuminated attendees and inspired them for many years to come with talking points that provided a balance of personal passion and technical brilliance. She leveraged the power of storytelling to invoke collaboration and inovation with her stakeholders.

What did these two luminaries do that was so remarkable? They captivated their listeners with *compelling content.* You may not realize it yet, but you can also engage people with strategic stories that will inform and inspire them.

Before I provide you with three content templates that will act as your presentation playbooks and help you achieve storytelling excellence, I'll share some general tips that will be beneficial on your journey to luminosity. I compare this process to picking at delectable appetizers before dining on the scrumptious main course and finishing it off with a delicious dessert. If you fill your presentation with the finest ingredients and cook your dishes with utmost care, precision, and passion, you will nourish and satiate the hearts and minds of your listeners.

Appetizers

My wife and I love trying new restaurants. When choosing a new place, we research things such as location, type of food, online reviews, menus, etc. By the time we sit down in an establishment, we're ready to eat because we've already reviewed relevant information about the meal.

Similarly, when it comes to content for technical presentations, we always want to share *context* before we share the actual messages (as modeled in the Table of Contents of this book). We need to explain to our audience some *background* on the goods before we serve them.

For each of the following snack-size appetizer tips, I've modeled the best practice about context by sharing brief *background* (research, anecdotes, etc.) before explaining how to apply the best practice to your daily communication in the form of guiding *bites* that you can easily snack on to nourish your content competence.

First Appetizer Tip: The Rule of Three

Background: Organizing information into lists of three is often the best way to convey messages. A basic principle of neuroscience is that our brains best recognize patterns in groups of three to help retain memory of them. When it comes to presentations, a list of three is less work for audience members. Unfortunately, some engineers tend to present the five, ten, or fifteen plus features of their technical work, which distract from the audience retaining their key messages. Think about the following key words from the Declaration of Independence: "Life, Liberty, and the Pursuit of Happiness." The phrase has become a recognizable part of American vernacular because it is so clean, simple, and memorable.

Bite: You can leverage this rule by distilling your main points into three primary categories. You may have seven important updates to share about your new AI model, for example, but, if you fold them into the three, higher-level topics (i.e. training, fine-tuning, and inference) your presentation becomes more commanding because no one is going to pay attention to laundry lists of information or remember excessive details. Keep your audience engaged by organizing the menu of your content into no more than three items.

Second Appetizer Tip: Simple Sound Bites

Background: Your goal as a speaker is to deliver your messages as succinctly as possible. As previously mentioned, too much information causes "cognitive overload" among listeners, not unlike a system that has a limited amount of data storage space. Use simple words and brief phrases wherever possible, as this approach also has greater impact. This quote from Nelson Mandela, the late President of South Africa, serves as a perfect example: "I greet you all in the name of peace, democracy, and freedom for all. I stand here before you not as a prophet, but as a humble servant of you, the people. Your tireless and heroic sacrifices have made it possible for me to be here today. I therefore place the remaining years of my life in your hands."

Bite: Whether speaking to rising nations or technical stakeholders, focus on sound bites for key messages to entice your audience efficiently. If you want your audience to grasp and embrace your ideas, shape them into the form of succinct points (five-ten words maximum). When creating talking points for your slides, imagine your audience nibbling at the most delectable pieces of your big talk. By creating simple memorable takeaways, you are creating light appetizers that are easy to consume, digest, and remember.

Third Appetizer Tip: Illustrative Language

Background: As you may have noticed throughout this book, I use a lot of illustrations. Having polled thousands of technical speakers after their training sessions, I discovered that many of them shared my affinity for using visual explanations to learn new concepts. This makes sense for two reasons: 1) ninety percent of information transmitted to the brain is visual; and 2) images are processed in the brain 60,000 times faster than the written word.

Bite: When crafting your slides, make them more visual and limit not only the number of bullets, but also the length of each line of text to no more than five words. This way, all the words are more visible and easier to read, and you have room for clean blank space. You and your content need to be the main focal points of your presentation—not the slides, which should be regarded as eye-pleasing, digestible, and supplemental. (For more specific guidance on slide design, I recommend Nancy Duarte's book *Resonate*.)

Similarly, as you are crafting talking points to coincide with the slides, try to use metaphors and analogies (in other words, comparisons) with illustrative language, so your audience can visualize concepts and retain them even better. For a good eample of how to use analogies in a real tech talk, search YouTube for "Breaking Magical Barriers" by VMware's Staff Engineer, Gerhard Lazu. Gerhard and I leveraged illustrative storytelling to craft a narrative about how his team pushed the maximum of a single replicated RabbitMQ queue from twenty-five thousand messages per second (mps) to one million mps, by connecting the work with Bugatti and how they pushed the maximum speed of their record-setting Chiron to break the 300mph barrier.

For a more simple approach to using illustrative language with technical content, here's a hypothetical example from Relli's tour:

> I'd now like you to follow me to my personal favorite part of the DC, our rack maintenance trains. This technology is responsible for maintaining and updating equipment in the DC, such as server machines, to ensure they're working properly. For those who aren't familiar with DC operations, you can think of maintenance trains as operating like freight trains because they routinely transport and manaage computer servers, which

are the core processors of our app data. They are highly productive as they travel from one region of a DC to another, to not just add new servers, but also help fix and replace old servers to keep everything running on track.

Fourth Appetizer Tip: Characters That Connect

Background: In 2012, James Chapman published an article in *Business Insider* that revealed the top ten most read books over the prior fifty years. The Bible placed first, followed by *Quotations from Mao Tse-Tung* as a distant second. You might have already guessed number three, which happens to be my wife's favorite: *Harry Potter*, by J.K. Rowling. I mention this novel for the simple reason that not only do people love great storytelling and fantastic settings, but they also get hooked because the author draws them into the characters. In *Harry Potter*, Rowling invented timeless recurring figures who connected with readers on an emotional level: brave heroes (Harry, Hermione, and Ron), rotten adversaries (Voldemort, Draco, and Professor Snape), and quirky allies (Professor Dumbledore, Dobby, and Hagrid). While it's unlikely you are crafting a work of fiction in your business presentation, you can still incorporate relatable characters into your storytelling to engage your audience.

Bite: Presenters can learn a great deal from how novelists fill their stories with magnetic characters. As you present your work and tell a story, you can share the contributions of key stakeholders who directly and indirectly impacted the positive outcomes. Your audience members will enjoy recognizing their peers, while those in the audience who were given special shoutouts will feel appreciated.

In addition to recognizing contributors, you can also identify other key characters involved in your work—decision makers, champions, partners, and any other relevant stakeholders—so that you can then cater your communication to them accordingly.

Fifth Appetizer Tip: Novelty

Background: I loved watching my kids when they were around four months old. At this stage, their alertness grew, and their eyes lit up whenever they noticed new things.

This phenomenon doesn't stop as we grow from childhood to adulthood. Shiny objects continue to capture our visual attention throughout our lives. If you doubt this fact, consider how many billboards you notice alongside roads and highways. You may be like most drivers who can't resist rubbernecking at accidents, even though this contributes even more to the traffic that annoyed you as you approached the scene.

Bite: Neuroscientific studies have shown that we are hardwired to enjoy novelty because we release dopamine—a powerful neurotransmitter that travels to the pleasure centers in our brains—each time we experience something new. During your presentations, you want to find ways to stimulate dopamine activity among your audience members (in a purely professional way, of course). You can accomplish this by highlighting what is new, exciting, and innovative about your pioneering ideas and/or approach to common problems. What aspects of your technical work are unique and distinctive from others to showcase their novelty and further engage your audience?

The Main Course

Now that we've been treated to some appetizing fundamentals, it's time to move to our main course, which consists of three content templates. The table below breaks down their distinctions to illustrate how you can create better content for various situations. Like any item on a menu, every meal is different: Some require few ingredients and are easier to prepare for basic enjoyment (practical), others involve intense preparation and feature extensive creativity for more flavorful enjoyment (engagement).

Template	Level of Practicality	Level of Engagement
Practical Plot	Most	Least
Story Formula	Moderate	Moderate
Hero's Journey	Least	Most

1st Template: Practical Plot

My daughters' favorite holiday movie is *The Grinch*, which means I watch it an average of forty-two times every year during the holiday season (and another fourteen the rest of the year). Although I always become annoyed from the Hooville carols getting stuck in my head, I have learned to appreciate the word wizardry of the author, Dr. Seuss. He had a unique talent for captivating audiences by his use of four key elements of storytelling: setting, characters, problem, and solution. These story elements can be useful for speakers to have on hand, especially when you must think on your feet…

For example, what would you do if your VP happened to join you for an elevator ride, during which she asked what you are working on? Many technical professionals I know can easily fill multiple hour-long coaching sessions with explanations about their work based on basic prompts. It's an entirely different story, however, when they must improvise and provide a powerful, succinct elevator update on the spot under pressure.

This is where the first content framework comes in, enabling you to leverage the simple story elements of Dr. Seuss to convey the essence of your work with logical appeal. The pitch can be addressed to anyone, but it must be especially tight for senior leaders who have shorter-than-average attention spans and tend to be allergic to too many technical details. As the table on the previous page shows, the Practical Plot is highly practical, especially when you need to share a high-level explanation about your work in a brief period. The following template helps you organize your content into the four elements of Dr. Seuss's storytelling formula:

1. The setting: *when/where/what*

2. The characters: *who*

3. The problem: *why*

4. The solution: *how*:

To bring this first template to life, let's start with *what not to do* in a hypothetical elevator discussion between Alice (a VP) and Bob (a developer who hadn't heard of the Practical Plot):

Alice: Hey, Bob, nice to see you. What are you working on these days?
Bob: I'm fine-tuning algorithms for our ML models using some open-source software that utilizes mixed integer informatics with different types of coding languages that are causing lots of problems for our infrastructure because no one knows how to use them like I do.

Do you think Alice was impressed by Bob's response? Unless she was working in the weeds with Bob on his work, I would say not. If anything, I think she was confused and hopped out of the elevator the next time the doors opened, even though it wasn't her floor.

Now let's look at Bob's revised response after considering Dr. Seuss' expertise with the Practical Plot:

Bob: Thanks for asking, Alice. In the beginning of the last half, we started working lower in the infrastructure stack on our cloud storage systems with our AI customers. Their inference models started having bad latency, so we've been developing automation protocols to increase efficiency.

Let's review the key elements that Bob touched on:

1. *When*: "beginning of the last half"

2. *Where*: "working lower in the infrastructure stack"

3. *What*: "cloud storage systems"

4. *Who*: "AI customers"

5. *Why*: "inference models started having bad latency…"

6. *How*: "developing automation protocols"

Sometimes the improved response will suffice, but there are other occasions where a senior leader might want a bit more information, as in the following:

Alice: *Wow, that sounds like exciting and complex work. I've been struggling to keep up with all of our AI efforts and worry that our GPU resources are being strained from the extensive ML workloads. Are you working with anyone else? How are the protocols coming along?*

This is where the lessons in Chapter Two—re: listening to analyze and adapt—come in. Alice just shared what's important to her based on the pain points she expressed ("struggling to keep up" and "worry that our GPU resources are being strained"), which could enable a good listener like Bob to craft his follow-up comments in a more sympathetic way.

Bob: *I hear you on all of the various AI efforts and their costs. Fortunately, we have a cross-functional team of people from different departments to co-design the many facets of this project—from data scientists and product leads to hardware and software developers. We're making good progress in our swim lanes, which is helping create the most efficient protocols for our inference customers. I'd be happy to share a status update at the next All Hands, if it'd be helpful for everyone to hear more about our collaborative progress.*

Alice: *Yes, that's a terrific idea! Please plan to do this, so we can keep up the momentum and maybe even find you some more engineering support for you.*

What did Bob do right? He capitalized on his elevator opportunity by not only adapting to his VP's perceived concerns, but also assuring her that the situation was under control, acknowledging the involvement of people from different departments, and volunteering to share updates with the wider organization.

As you can see, the Practical Plot provides a simplified outline that you can populate based on the key elements of your projects. You can then adjust or expand as needed on the fly, depending on your audience and objectives.

Light Up Ventures and the Practical Plot

Many of the technical leaders who join our coaching sessions do so because they're participating in a company-sponsored engagement, so

---

SIDECAR

Although you may need to add more details to the Practical Plot, always keep your messaging succinct—especially when communicating with a senior leader. If she asks a question, it's not an invitation to back up the dump truck on her. Brevity creates levity, which lightens the burden on your listener's brain.

they don't know much about Light Up Ventures and often ask our trainers what we do. Let's see what the Practical Plot looks like in action from a broader company perspective to provide a real-world example for a business, in case you're working on something similar for your company...

- Our *who*: From Fortune 50s to agencies and nonprofits, Light Up Ventures partners with individuals, teams, and organizations.

- Our *what*: We provide certified coaching and training opportunities focused on leadership development with an emphasis on communication competence.

- Our *how*: Our services differ from others based on our unique expertise matched with four servant leadership, masterful guidance, and compassionate creativity.

- Our *why*: Our hearts experience pain when we see disengaged professionals who suffer in darkness from lifeless leadership and boring communications, so we aim to develop leaders and brighten their world with our illuminating work.

2nd Template: Story Formula

The next template, the Story Formula, may become your new best friend at work because it helps you easily present your work in day-to-day communications with minimal preparation and strong effectiveness. Whether you want your audience to *do* and/or *feel* something, the formula provides a cohesive structure to convey your messages in a way that best achieves your objectives.

Can you guess how many sections this framework contains? If

your mind immediately leapt to the number three because of the third appetizer tip—the rule of three, cited earlier—you're tracking well on your journey to luminosity.

The number three is powerful because every good story consists of that many parts, identified as the *beginning*, the *middle*, and the *end*. In the figure below, you will find a visual representation of the formula in which the inputs—beginning/middle/end—produce the output of effective engagement.

We are now going to break down the formula and transform the key elements into the main sections of technical stories: the Intro, the Middle, and the Close.

Effective Engagement (Achieve Objectives with Audience)		
=		
Logos +	Ethos +	Pathos
Problematic Intro (Personal Hook + Historical Context)	Innovative Main Messages^3 (Necessity + Complexity + Novelty)	Inspiration Close (Results + Future Work + Takeaways)

The "Problematic" Intro: Set the Stage

Technical audience members are usually curious people who love learning about hard problems, but are also busy, with limited attention spans, so they need to be enticed immediately and have their expectations set by speakers at the beginning of the presentation. The outline addresses those considerations in the form of three things, which we'll address individually: the hook, context, and preview.

The Hook: The key to starting your presentation strong is a thoughtful hook. This requires some level of creativity to grab your audience in a personal way; otherwise, they will tune out. You might present a brief piece of intriguing research that you find especially compelling or an impressive little-known statistic to teach your audience something new while demonstrating your passion for the work.

Another option is to pose a challenging question to your audience that inspires reflection. Or you can make the exchange interactive by inviting them to participate in a simple exercise, such as "Raise your hand if you know how many AI startups launched last year."

> **SIDECAR**
>
> Any time you are communicating with people–especially technical professionals, who love to learn–try to teach them something new with relevant insights they likely don't know.

Provocative statements or visual demonstrations, such as those employed by Steve Jobs, have the potential to wow an audience. Carmine Gallo identified the following as Principle Five in his bestseller *The Presentation Secrets of Steve Jobs*: "Create insanely different experiences." This refers as much to presentations as it does to extraordinary customer service, which is helpful to keep in mind, since we should view our audience as customers we serve.

Personal anecdotes and humor can sometimes be strong tactics for establishing a human connection with your audience at the start. Note that I did the former in the opening of Chapter Four with a personal story, where I shared the tragic passing of my late friend, Chachi, to set up my following message about living purposefully.

A few words of caution about the latter technique are necessary here. Before you attempt any humor, you must be one hundred percent certain you know your audience and understand their sensitivities. A joke can be particularly risky. If it works, you'll have people eating out of the palm of your hand. If it bombs, however, you may not be able to recover from the audience reaction (or lack thereof, such

Craft Content—Part Two 117

as crickets). There are few things more uncomfortable than watching a speaker squirm on stage after having told a joke that offended someone, involved something cliché, or just hit the stage with a thud. If you have any doubt about incorporating humor, test it out in advance on someone who represents the audience and can provide objective feedback.

Context: The second aspect of introductions in the Story Formula is context. As mentioned earlier in the Appetizers section, you must establish credibility and common ground before diving into the details of your work in the middle of your presentation. Providing adequate background information with historical context upfront helps establish a narrative and brings everyone up to speed. Providing background info can also proactively help you avoid interruptions in the middle of your presentation. Unfortunately, some audiences include a know-it-all who wants to prove her or his intelligence by asking blunt—and sometimes obnoxious—questions to disrupt the flow of meetings. If, however, you provide ample context from the start, you can prevent these distractions from surfacing or at least table them until the end of your presentation, giving yourself enough time to come up with a composed response.

Keep in mind if you happen to lead a daily scrum with the same regular team members, you probably don't need to give as much context because your audience is well versed with your content. In this case, you don't want to waste anyone's time on details they already know. Your best bet is to start the scrum with a terse statement summing up the situation, such as: "We all know we're stuck—let's *unstick*."

However, if you're kicking off a new project with a cross-functional group, you must ensure that everyone is starting out on the same page with several baseline points to provide ample context. These might include things such as:

Past context with key milestones of how you determined the need for the project.

- The project's overarching vision and goals.

- A clear statement of the problem you are trying to solve.

- Benefits and potential opportunities stemming from the initiative.

- References to a similar project, if one exists.

- Clarity around roles and responsibilities.

- Specific benchmarks and deadlines.

- Identification of real and/or potential threats and challenges that might be obstacles.

- Mention of previous attempts or failures to solve the problem and share why those solutions were insufficient.

- Any other contextual points to help build up the *what/why/who* in the intro of your story before transitioning to the *how* in the middle.

By sharing the above out of the gate, you are educating, informing, and motivating the group while also starting with clarity (*logos*), which earns the audience's trust. At the same time, you are validating your own leadership and proving you have command of the situation.

The one potential pitfall: Sometimes busy senior executives decide to make a surprise appearance halfway into a presentation. Kind leaders will sit, smile, and listen, holding their questions until the end. The self-absorbed, controlling ones jump right in with tough questions they wouldn't have had to ask if they'd been in attendance from the beginning when you provided context.

I've been in this awkward situation many times myself. It can seem overwhelming, especially if you're young and ambitious and want to prove yourself. A human reaction to this situation is to become nervous and anxious, which can cause you to stumble and lose your place. Sometimes you feel the need to start your presentation all over again from the beginning for just that one person, which frustrates everyone else in the room. My suggestion in these circumstances is to take a deep breath, remain calm and focused, and answer the executive's question as concisely as possible with just the topline, key points. Repeat as little as possible and don't try to embarrass the leader by lobbing back a semi-snarky statement, such as "Oh, I covered that already." Never try to overreach and share unsubstantiated information, which gives the executive room to correct and undermine you in front of your peers. If you truly don't know the answer, honesty is always best: "Thanks for bringing up this important topic. I don't have that information handy and would like to provide a verified answer. Is it ok if I research it and get back to you with a response?"

Preview: This is the last component of the beginning of your talk. The *preview* is exactly as it sounds: a way for attendees to prepare themselves for what is to come.

You could create a formal bare bones agenda slide or verbally introduce the three main sections— keep your agenda to only one or two key messages but not more than three—that will appear in the middle of your talk. By doing this, you are letting the audience know that their time will be well spent. Gurus such as Dale Carnegie famously taught, "Tell the audience what you're going to say, say it; then tell them what you've said." This summary of the beginning, middle, and end of your talk is helpful for a simple approach to driving retention of your main messages through repetition.

One final way to hook your audience: *teasing*. This is a more enticing form of previewing that can also help with signposting, which we covered in prior chapters and was exemplified by my Alcatraz tour guide.

By teasing your audience with an exciting hint of what is to come (such as the mysterious story about Al Capone during the Alcatraz stop), you are giving your audience a reason to perk up and stick around until the end. In the earlier story in the elevator involving Alice (the VP), Bob secured an opportunity to present his team's work to the broader organization at their upcoming All Hands. During the presentation, he could have hooked his audience's attention by sharing a fun fact about the number of AI startups from the prior year and some basic context about their cloud storage project. He then could have teased the most exciting part of their work in his preview: "Later in my update, I'll share how our novel approach to inference increased modeling speed by twelve percent."

The "Meaty" Middle: Showcase the Work

Before we explore what happens in the middle section, it's important for us to note the importance of *transitions* in a presentation. These are essential for seamless storytelling because they serve as logical bridges, providing a natural passage from one message or section to the next. Without transitions, your presentation risks being disorganized and choppy. There are certain transitory phrases you can use to help provide segues when needed:

- Now that I've provided background context, we can move on to details about _____...

- While we're on the subject of _____...

- Let's shift gears a bit and talk about _____...

Once you have transitioned to the middle (or "meat") of your talk, consider these best practices to make sure the Story Formula functions properly by providing the core substance about your work:

- Focus on necessity, complexity, and novelty to highlight the innovation of your work and connect with ethos—credibility. Drive home why your work is so important, challenging, and unique.

- Where it makes sense, try to stimulate conflict or tension to keep your audience engaged. Think about your favorite films and how their directors developed tension to keep you on the edge of your seat. For tech talks, consider building up the complexity of your problem space by elaborating on the pain of challenges to draw your engineering audience in. Simply highlighting the "before" and "after" of your technical projects can showcase contrast and resolution.

- Take a page from presidential speech writers and leverage the power of repetition, which fosters retention and adds emphasis. Be mindful of redundancy while at the same time tying a common thread throughout your presentation. Repeating key messages helps audiences remember your work in a cohesive manner.

- Always utilize the rule of three to convey your key subsections of content in the middle of your presentation. When crafting these middle messages, condense the most crucial topics and ditch the rest. Be strict on what makes the cut. Some examples: Explain the past, present, and future; cite the problem, solution, and impact; or share a challenge, opportunity, and strategy.

- Convey your main points as sound bites (noted in the above "Appetizers") as in this statement from Google CEO Sundar Pichai: "Google teams have lots of autonomy, including from people like me."

- Strike a balance between presenting objective information as well as subjective opinion. If you're running a live demo, be concise by citing tangible benefits rather than itemizing a laundry list of features. If you highlighted a surprising obstacle that came up while trying to solve a problem, be vulnerable by sharing failures that led to insightful learnings and future success.

- Build up a narrative about your work that conveys the evolution of its ongoing progress by gradually moving from one phase or milestone of your project to the next to showcase constant iteration and innovation.

The Concluding Close: Wrap It Up

Neuroscience emphasizes the importance of primacy and recency for communication effectiveness. Audiences remember what they heard at the beginning and end of a speaker's presentation. After starting strong with your intro and constantly re-engaging your audience throughout the middle, you can now finish strong with your closing comments. The simplest approach is to offer clear capsule takeaways that highlight your most important points to help you achieve your overall objectives for the presentation. Wherever possible, leverage the rule of three. Cite the things that have the greatest measurable impact or will allude to forward momentum by sharing future initiatives with an inspirational tone connecting to the pathos part of communication—emotional conviction. Ending with measurable results followed by a roadmap of future challenges closes the loop on your overall narrative. Looping full circle back to your beginning remarks—which we will cover more in depth at the end of the chapter—can be particularly effective. Depending on your subject and the scope of the initiative, you might be able to close with action items or topics for further discussion. Hopefully, by the end of your presentation, you've left at least one-third of your total time for the audience to ask a few questions. In Chapter Nine, we'll share some tips for improving Q&A (question and answer) competence.

As icing on the cake after Q&A, you want to conclude with a memorable line that drives home your main message. Steve Jobs, for example, concluded his 2007 iPhone speech with the following:

> *There's an old Wayne Gretzky quote that I love. "I skate to where the puck is going to be, not where it has been." And we've always tried to do that at Apple. Since the very very beginning. And we always will. So, thank you very very much for being a part of this.*

Whether you are launching products to consumers around the world or listing problems to colleagues at work, add the Story Formula to your communications arsenal. A practical outline will help you achieve objectives with any audience. The sequential storytelling of this format combines the beginning (set the stage); the middle (showcase the work); and the end (wrap it up) to take your presentation prowess to new heights. If you're interested in seeing how this formula functions in real tech talks, check out the @Scale conference website (atscaleconference.com). The site houses a library of content based on our storytelling guidance, with top speakers from around the industry to showcase their innovative work on the most complex technical challenges at hyper scale.

The Hero's Journey

In dramatic storytelling—whether it's a film, TV show, play, or novel—the main character undergoes a series of challenges on her or his way toward accomplishing a desired goal. This concept of storytelling was first introduced by Aristotle in his masterwork *Poetics*. Later, it was explored by psychologist Carl Jung and mythology expert Joseph Campbell, who created one of the most powerful storytelling frameworks, "the hero's journey."

A hero's journey should be something that resonates on a deep level with an audience. If the character, quest, and story are compelling enough, people are cheering for her or him to succeed. Producer/director George Lucas, familiar with Joseph Campbell's work, tailored the concept as he developed the *Star Wars* franchise. What moviegoer wasn't all in for Luke Skywalker's heroic journey to rescue Princess Leah and become a Jedi?

For business presentations, I like to reference Donald Miller's *Building a StoryBrand*. In the book, he offers seven elements based on hero's journey ideology that may be applied to successfully marketing brands. I've condensed and simplified them here for your technical presentations with examples of how they appear in *Star Wars* and then tailored to how they could be used in your technical presentations.

1. A *hero* or protagonist is the person (or people) who chooses a desirable and relatable goal. He or she faces internal and/or external conflicts while embarking on a quest to achieve this important outcome. (Will the underdog sports team win the championship? Will the guy get the girl? Will the startup change the world?) Often the hero has a "character arc" in which the character learns and grows from the challenging experiences along the journey.

- *Star Wars:* Luke Skywalker's goal of rescuing the Princess and becoming a Jedi are associated with even higher stakes—saving the universe.

- *Your presentation:* Surprise! We, as presenters, are not the heroes. The heroes are your stakeholders who are likely in the audience—whether they're senior decision makers or fellow IC contributors. They all have desires associated with your work that make them your heroic stakeholders: resolve technical issues, develop new technology, reach quarterly goals, improve product engagement, etc.

2. The *villain(s)* is the antagonist (opponent) or stumbling block; it could be anyone or anything that serves as the main obstacle in the way of heroes achieving their desires.

    - *Star Wars:* This is represented by the Evil Empire and its army of antagonists, such as Darth Vader, the Emperor, and the Storm Troopers.

    - *Your presentation:* The villain might be a difficult decision maker in the organization or an outside competitor. Generally, however, the "villains" for technical projects aren't people, but rather the obstacles that get in the way of accomplishing the goals: lack of resources, latent services, bugs in the system, etc.

3. The *guide(s)* is an expert with experience and wisdom to mentor and direct the hero on his or her journey to overcome the villains and achieve their desires.

- *Star Wars:* Han Solo, Yoda, and Obi-Wan Kenobe have unique expertise and relevant perspectives to guide Luke on his journey.

- *Your presentation:* This is where you come in. As the speaker, you position yourself as a guide to share how your work will help audience members overcome their technical obstacles and achieve their goals.

4. *A plan* is the strategy on how the hero and his guide(s) will defeat the villain(s) and achieve the goal.

    - *Star Wars:* The rebel pilots review plans of the Death Star with their leaders to devise a strategy for destroying it, while Luke also undergoes intense training with his mentors to become a Jedi.

    - *Your presentation:* As a guide, you propose the plan that will help the heroes overcome the villain(s) and achieve the goal. This could be more technical, such as a plan to evolve a system's architecture or more project-based, such as timelines to take a product from beta to production. The best guides facilitate collaboration and are open to input on their plans from others, so their guidance is received better. Remember Obi-Wan's servant leadership: He sacrificed himself to help Luke continue his hero's journey and discover his own destiny.

5. and 6. *Potential doom* and *possible gains* are the two things that represent what's at stake for the hero in terms of failure versus success.

- *Star Wars:* Potential doom means that Luke fails his training, and the Evil Empire conquers the universe. Success means that Luke masters the Force to protect the good side and provide freedom for all galactic citizens.

- *Your presentation:* This is where you create dramatic tension and a bit of fear by presenting what's at stake if the plan doesn't succeed: technical debt, system outages, product latency, missed KPIs, unhappy customers, etc. At the same time, you're motivating them and negating the fear by highlighting what success (impact) looks like: increased platform adoption, better developer productivity, streamlined processes, new features, cost savings, happy customers, etc.

7. *Call everyone to action* is when the hero understands everything that's at stake (usually within the first nine minutes of any movie) and it becomes time for the hero to embark on their journey while viewers embark on their next bowl of popcorn.

- *Star Wars:* Luke and his extended allies—the best pilots in the Rebel Alliance—unite behind the strategy and shoot out into space to destroy the Death Star and defeat the Evil Empire while he embarks on his personal journey of becoming a Jedi.

- *Your presentation:* Lastly, after showing how your work (plan) will help your stakeholders achieve their goals (heroes w/ desires), you invite them to embark on a journey with you as their technical lead (guide). You are motivating the team with action items (next steps, approvals, tasks, etc.) and guidance that will help the key stakeholders assemble, follow the plan, and defeat the enemy (challenging obstacles).

To land the plane of this final content template with one more brief example, here's a graphic representing the hero's journey, as applied to a hypothetical example of technical security work.

Hero's Journey-Framework

Story Element	Security Examples
1. Hero w/ Desires	Customer seeking solution to their security needs
2. Villain	Obstacles to strong security posture
3. Guide	Security System Lead/Presenter
4. Plan	Details of security solution with specifics about addressing customer's obstacles
5. Potential Doom	Security threats that cause worse problems for broader business
6. Potential Value	Successful security posture supporting broader user/business impact
7. Call to Action	Questions, discussion, follow up meetings, etc. (situational per presentation)

Dessert

A good meal is incomplete without something sweet to finish things off. With that in mind, here's the cherry on top of storytelling techniques—*looping*, which resolves the tension you can create by *teasing* in the intro of your talk (referenced earlier in the chapter). This is when you introduce a morsel in the beginning of your talk and then wrap back around to it at the end—hence, "closing the loop." For example, I opened this chapter with Steve Jobs' speech in which he introduced three revolutionary products. However, if you turn the pages back, you'll notice I included the first part of his quote (where he teased about "...introducing three revolutionary products...") but left you hanging about what he said next. I'll now *loop* back around now and provide his next talking points, which changed the world:

> *These are not three separate devices. These are one device. And we're calling it the iPhone."*

Another way to put a bow on your presentation is to end with a well-chosen, snack-sized quote. It could be inspirational, amusing, prescriptive, or reflective, but it must tie into the theme of your presentation, as modeled by the closing of Steve Jobs' presentation, which I shared earlier where he referenced Wayne Gretzky.

To model this technique before closing with takeaways, I'll leave you with one final piece of inspiration from filmmaker Steven Spielberg:

> *The most amazing thing for me is that every single person who sees a movie, not necessarily one of my movies, brings a whole set of unique experiences, but through careful manipulation and good storytelling, you can get everybody to clap at the same time, to hopefully laugh at the same time, and to be afraid at the same time.*

Takeaways

- When creating a presentation, think of it in terms of a three-course meal: appetizer, entrée, and dessert.

- Use the rule of three, sound bites, and illustrative language wherever possible in your presentation.

- Utilize the Practical Plot by answering *where, what, who, why,* and *how.*

- Every good story has a beginning, middle, and end that you can craft by leveraging the StoryFormula template.

- For a more powerful approach to storytelling, take your audience on a thrilling journey that features a hero with a goal, a villain, a guide, a plan, potential doom, possible gains, and a call to action.

ACT III

Story*telling*—The *How*

CHAPTER SEVEN

Deliver Deliberately—Part One

In his bestselling book *Talk Like TED*, Carmine Gallo references an intriguing court case study as he emphasizes the importance of nonverbal communication to prepare TED Talk speakers. In the study, three distinct groups of jurors were responsible for evaluating the validity of a suspect's testimony. The first group, which only had access to the *audio* portion of a case interview file, had a fifty-five percent success rate in determining the validity of the suspect's testimony based purely on what they heard. The second group of jurors—which didn't have any audio access but was able to view the suspect's body language on *video*—had a sixty-five percent success rate. The third and final group, which was able to review *both audio and video* of the suspect's testimony, had an eighty-five percent success rate.

I'm sure you've figured out on your own the conclusion from the above study, but I'll state it anyway: While verbal and non-verbal communication elements have impact individually, they have even more influence on audiences when they are combined for compounded impact.

This result harkens back to the 1960 presidential debate between John F. Kennedy and Richard Nixon. The people who listened to the debate on the radio thought Nixon won; those who viewed it on television believed that Kennedy was the victor. From a visual perspective, Kennedy was young, handsome, and poised, whereas Nixon—who perspired profusely and kept checking the clock—came across as nervous and shifty. Kennedy ultimately won the election, which was in no small part due to his more favorable physical presence and body language on camera.

In previous sections, we covered the essentials of understanding our audiences, defining objectives, and crafting content. We'll now complete the equation with our fourth and final variable. Once you stand in front of an audience, you must also master the art of *delivering deliberately* which, in simple terms, refers to *how* you express yourself. We'll begin with some supportive context about why this variable is important before moving on to practical guidance in the next chapter.

The tenor of your voice can send a powerful positive or negative signal, whether intentional or not. For example, if your child or roommate leaves a mess in the kitchen, your first inclination might be to yell her or his name across the house in an accusatory tone, which lets the person automatically know in advance, "Uh oh, I'm in trouble…"

When you are a presenter, audiences pick up the on the slightest nuance of both *what* you are saying and *how* you are saying it. If, for example, you confidently assert that a project is one hundred percent on schedule and speak with an optimistic tone about its probable success, your audience will be more inclined to believe you. However, if you forget your place, garble words, speak too softly, repeat phrases, or take awkward pauses, they will assume you're nervous and interpret these signs as a lack of competence. When this occurs, the audience loses faith in your ability as a speaker and doubts the validity of the points you're trying to get across—no matter how on target they might be.

From my experience, individuals who leverage the benefits of *intentional delivery* reap the rewards. They win over audiences, garner trust, leave favorable, lasting impressions and, most importantly, ensure that their messages are understood and well received.

Tune Your Parameters

While I'm far from an AI expert, I happen to find machine learning fascinating. Back in 2023, I had the privilege of advising an AI startup just as the massive wave was forming. I was intrigued by one concept that gave the startup a unique competitive advantage: *parameter tuning*. Without getting into the technical weeds, my basic understanding of the intent of parameter tuning is to improve a model's performance by selecting the best values for its parameters. By fine-tuning the parameters, data scientists and researchers can achieve better results, reduce errors, and optimize the overall performance of their models.

Nonverbal communication bears some similarity to parameter tuning in the sense that it also involves factors that determine the effectiveness of your content output. Before we dive into utilizing parts of your body to improve your public speaking performance, we'll review some relevant data that I briefly showed in the Introduction of this book.

The graphic on the next page illustrates the results of a famous study on nonverbal communication conducted by Dr. Mehrabian in the 1960s. In the decades since, there have been many critiques on the methodology and the favorability of the results, which is perfectly okay, as we won't be consuming the "whole pie." We'll take two bites of it and leave the rest.

The pie chart reveals various parameters of nonverbal communication representing the weight of words (content) in contrast to how the words were physically expressed (delivery). The first thing you probably noticed is the glaring low percentage (seven percent) for "spoken words," which indicates how little people pay attention to what we say. This is something of a wake-up call for speakers to recognize that the words don't matter as much as they think. Bear in mind that this doesn't negate the previous two chapters in this book about the importance of content development. However, it makes an invaluable statement about the need to place greater emphasis on how we *look* and *sound* as the words come out of our mouths.

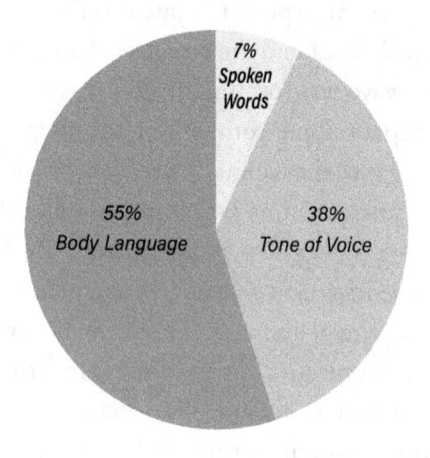

7% Spoken Words
55% Body Language
38% Tone of Voice

There's another vital factor not considered in the seven percent: In my experience, technical audiences tend to be laser-focused on details and what they need to know or can learn. Brilliant ICs tend to have an allergic reaction to overly charismatic senior leaders who wave their hands on stage but don't provide meaningful substance. Many engineers prefer a direct, no b.s. approach. I admit that I too have a personal distaste for excessive rah-rah cheerleading during presentations.

That said, if a speaker's vocalization and body language are poor, it doesn't matter how compelling the content might be. Even the most analytical, specialized audience will tune out. Like parameter tuning to optimize AI models, increasing the weight of importance on various delivery tactics will help optimize your presentation performance by grabbing and retaining your audience's attention while remaining authentic to your personal style.

We'll cover authenticity in the next chapter, but for now, think about delivery skills in terms of different levers that will help customize your presentation effectiveness. I encourage you to experiment with different options to determine which ones work best for you.

You can also think of delivery customization regarding my childhood heroes from *Star Wars*. If you are trying to help your audience problem solve by presenting deep technical complexity with many uncertainties, interdependencies, and constraints, go with the more robotic C-3PO approach to keep your messaging structured and logical. If, however, you are introducing bold ideas and innovations, think about how Han Solo might captivate and inspire the room.

Appear Confident

Most technical speakers I've worked with seem perfectly at ease when we're workshopping their presentations in a casual coaching session. It's an entirely different story when we move to the next phase, rehearsing—especially if the stakes are high. The shift from "conversation" to "presentation" mode inevitably causes butterflies to start fluttering in our stomachs, our cheeks to turn red as words come stuttering out of them, and our hearts to sound like Ewok drumbeats. The "fight-or-flight" response—originally intended to help protect us against physical threats—is our nervous system's way of reacting to fear and stress. When we make presentations, fight-or-flight is often triggered by the anxiety that comes from worrying about our performance.

Unfortunately, we can't always control how our brains and bodies will respond to pressure. However, by improving your delivery skills, you can appear with an air of confidence—no matter how shaky you might feel on the inside, while avoiding the unappetizing trait of arrogance. Before we share extensive guidance in the next chapter to improve your skills, let's start with a few simple reminders.

The Eyes: Windows to the Soul

Picture these three scenarios:

1. The speaker looks down at her feet throughout her presentation.

2. The speaker turns her back to the audience and speaks to her slides on a screen while she presents.

3. The speaker looks directly into the eyes of various audience members while occasionally referencing her slides on the screen.

In the above examples, which speaker is going to seem the most confident? Number three, of course, because she had engaging eye contact with most of her listeners. (It doesn't have to be with everyone.) Speaker number one will come across as timid and nervous while looking down during her presentation, which will detract from her perceived confidence. Meanwhile, speaker number two will lose connection with her audience because she's missing the opportunity to converse with them instead of the screen.

When it comes to eye contact, I've discovered there are two types of people: the speakers who enjoy it and focus on a few friendly faces, which strategically blurs out everyone else, and those who have difficulty looking at anyone in an audience because eye contact can be intimidating. If you fall into the second camp, I have a quick tip. Forget about looking into anyone's eyes; instead, focus on their foreheads, which gives the *appearance* of eye contact. You will avoid the difficulty of eye contact while appearing confident because your audience believes you are engaging with them.

Conviction and Composure

What adjectives come to mind when you picture the likeness of Dr. Martin Luther King Jr. standing firm and addressing a quarter of a million people at the Lincoln Memorial on August 28, 1963? The master orator may suggest many things, but I think most people would agree that his expression always communicates two traits above all: *conviction* and *composure*.

Conviction refers to when you believe in something so strongly you would go to great lengths to defend it. *Composure* is a state of seeming calm, cool, and collected in terms of how one holds him or herself in any situation, including times of stress. When these two words are used in tandem to describe a person, it automatically conjures up someone who deserves your attention and respect.

Dr. King humbly exuded these attributes, despite battling enormous pressure as he carried the weight of the civil rights movement on his shoulders and withstood constant threats against his life. His commitment to the cause was inspiring. Standing firm on his beliefs led him to sacrificing his life, which was taken from him when he was only thirty-nine years of age. If he had a chance to do it all over again, there is little doubt that he would keep to his convictions and remain composed until the end.

Powerful Presence

When I look back to my many years of working with thousands of tech leaders, there are a few who stand out above the rest. One such person is Vish Balachandran, who grew up in India and is now executive director and product engineering leader at Comcast.

I initially met Vish through our executive coaching work several years ago when he was a product leader at Amazon. We've since become good friends. I look back at our sessions with fondness because of Vish's commitment to his personal growth. He already had a strong foundation of natural confidence, so we were able to build on that by strengthening his executive presence—especially his composure. Whether presenting bleeding-edge innovations to Comcast's president or working on global telecommunications challenges with solution architects, Vish has learned to remain composed by embodying a relaxed, yet professional demeanor to empower a tangible sense of fearlessness.

If you're thinking, "That's great for Vish and high-up overlords, but I'm content as an IC and don't plan to climb the corporate ladder," I hear and applaud you for sticking to your particular plans. However, like Obi-Wan Kenobi did with Luke, I will encourage you to watch out for enemies who try to overpower you with bureaucratic bullying in corporate environments, and when necessary, stand your ground with recognizable confidence. If you know you struggle when it comes to confident body language, reflect on a study from Amy Cuddy's book, *Presence*, where social psychologists Dana Carney and Judith Hall, who carefully identified the behaviors of powerful people who "initiate handshakes, make more and longer eye contact, use broader gestures, have erect and open posture, lean forward and orient the body and head toward others, and are animated and self-assured in their physical expressions." These are potentially powerful weapons to be wielded with caution while remembering to always remain humble and kind.

Awareness

Try this quick exercise: Close your eyes, take a breath, and reflect on a recent meeting where you spoke. Answer the following questions as accurately and objectively as you can:

1. *What were your hands doing?*

2. *How was your posture?*

3. Where were you looking?

4. Were you standing still or shifting around?

From my experience, most people tend to falter when it comes to awareness of their physical presence. It's far too easy to be oblivious to what we look like standing in front of a group of people. We all have at least one nervous tic—a movement or sound—that seems innocuous right up until we start speaking in front of a group of people. Suddenly, when all eyes are upon us, the tiniest habit becomes a focal point for audience members and detracts from our presentation. Anything done excessively will be picked up by an audience; in some cases, it can even elicit jokes behind your back. Among the most common issues I've noticed: fidgeting (rocking/bouncing/swaying), excessive filler words, head tilting, stroking fingers through hair, eye darting, face rubbing, placing hands in pockets, foot tapping, playing with water bottles, chair swiveling, cackling strangely, lip smacking, breathing heavily into the microphone, and so on.

Yes, I admit that I had a nervous tic years ago: nail biting. I didn't think anything of it until I saw someone biting his nails in a meeting and thought it was disgusting and distracting. Once I became aware of my issue, I made a conscious effort and stopped it.

In the spirit of developing your self-awareness, let's refer to the figure on page 144. As you'll note when we review the three aspects of presentation delivery in the next chapter, everything below the middle line is what we want to stop doing. Like bugs in code, there are unhealthy tendencies in our nonverbal communication that we want to catch and remove. Once we cut bad habits, such as filler words and rocking our hips, we can progress to a baseline. This is a great place from which to develop your presentation skills because you are no longer distracting as a speaker. You've debugged the awkward tendencies and can maintain reasonable presence.

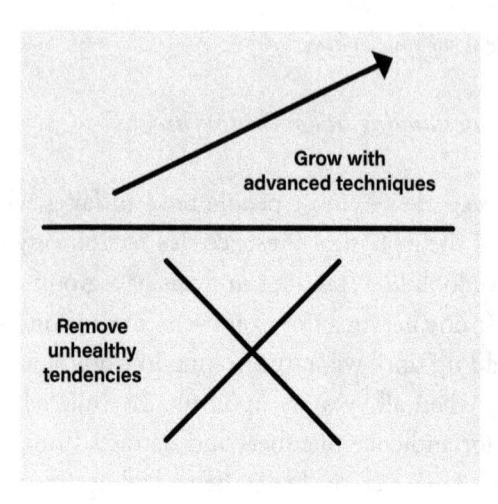

Lastly, we move above the line to master advanced delivery techniques. In most of our training sessions, many presenters start by considering what's below the line. From this point, they can advance and truly captivate their audiences with advanced delivery techniques operating above the line.

We'll cover practical tips about how to reduce one of the most common below-the-line pitfalls—*filler words*—in the next chapter but, for now, it's important to recognize how detrimental they can be to your delivery. Words such as *um, you know, sorta, er, like, uh, so, kinda* have no meaning and diminish the value of your content, signaling a lack of confidence in yourself and what you have to say. They're called filler words because the unnecessarily fill space in our speech. People who default to these words tend to drop them in every several seconds, which tests the patience of even the most supportive audience.

Perseverance

Before this chapter draws to a close, I would like to impart a confidence booster because, after reading about the pitfalls of delivery, you may be feeling self-conscious or discouraged.

--- SIDECAR ---

It's not so easy to identify our own tics. Sometimes our minds trick us into having wishful thoughts such as "I'm perfectly fine up there—I don't do anything weird when I present." On other occasions, we feel so embarrassed by what we might discover that we avoid facing the issue.

It's always a good idea to identify and correct any potential issues before you address an audience. Once you achieve self-awareness, problems become easier to correct.

One way to approach this is to study a recording of yourself on your phone as you rehearse your presentation. The most effective method is to find a trusted colleague, friend, or relative who can provide honest feedback and/or videotape your presentation for you to review.

If any tics are brought to light, face them head on. Do not ignore or dismiss them. If you or someone else picked up on them, treat the information as if you've been gifted with a courtesy. It's kind of like someone telling you that you have spinach between your teeth, salad dressing on your chin, or an open fly zipper. At the very least, ask a colleague or audio technician to check your physical appearance before you start speaking to ensure you're buttoned up.

You have the potential to become a confident speaker.
I'm not going to give you some empty pep talk and try to convince you that you'll conquer your fears and remove your tics overnight. However, I can say that I "see you" and empathize with your discomfort. Don't worry if you've had some rocky experiences in the past or even if your next presentation doesn't go exactly as planned. The key is to always show up, experiment in safe places, learn from missteps, and observe noticeable progress over time. You have the power within you to hold your head up high and ultimately win over any audience with powerful confidence.

In the meantime, I'll leave you with the following advice from social psychologist Amy Cuddy and her book *Presence*: "Fake it until you *become* it."

Takeaways

- Be aware that audiences pick up the on the slightest nuances of both *what* you are saying and *how* you are saying it.

- Use intentional delivery tactics to grab and retain your audience's attention while remaining authentic to your personal style.

- Employ good eye contact with at least a few audience members to help convey confidence.

- Practice *conviction* and *composure* to help command an audience's attention with *executive presence*.

- Become aware of every tic—physical and/or verbal—that might derail your presentation.

- Persevere! Believe in the potential to build your confidence and create a favorable rhythm for future opportunities.

CHAPTER EIGHT

Deliver Deliberately—Part Two

For four decades, late MIT Professor Patrick Winston delivered a talk titled "How to Speak" every January. Since the video was posted to YouTube in 2019, the talk has amassed nearly twenty million views.

Why has this lecture become so popular? Professor Winston offers numerous insightful problem-solving shortcuts or tips (referred to as *heuristics*) that he employs throughout his lecture. He begins by offering a powerful heuristic to his audience: *the empowerment promise*, a statement of what he vows to deliver to the audience by the time the presentation is over.

An effective communicator reads the minds of her or his audiences, anticipating their wants, needs, and expectations (as discussed in Chapters One and Two). An intriguing luminary introduces a succinct, compelling promise up front that connects with those desires. Once people are fully engaged, it becomes the speaker's responsibility to deliver the goods by the end of the session.

Here is my commitment to empower you for this chapter: I promise to provide practical tips that will improve your presentation delivery skills and strengthen your confidence as a speaker. I'm also committing to share a few more of Winston's tips with you and a link to his video by the end of this chapter.

With these promises in mind, please program your Jedi VR headset to the Millennium Falcon's cockpit as we begin our journey into delivery skills with instruction on authenticity.

Adaptive Yet Authentic

In previous chapters, I referenced such luminaries as the Hidden Figures, Elon Musk, Li Zheng, and Vish Balachandran—all of whom exemplify authentic delivery. The term *authenticity* is thrown around a lot these days, but what does it really mean?

In simple terms, luminaries speak with natural authority about what they know from their unique viewpoints. While they are able to adapt to their audiences (covered in Chapters One and Two), they don't copy others, conform to what other speakers are doing around them, provide cookie cutter commentary, or say anything that might sacrifice their personal integrity. While it can be helpful to pick up a few techniques and tricks from people you admire—both public figures and those you know personally—it's more important that you always remain true to yourself. If you are ever in doubt about whether you're crossing the line, ask yourself these questions: *Would I really say that? Would I really say it that way? Is there a chance that my audience won't believe I am credible and/or trustworthy if I emulate that other person's speaking style?*

One of my favorite things about the Millenium Falcon ship is how people often misjudge its capabilities right away based on appearance alone; characters in the films often dismiss it as a pile of junk. While the ship's rugged exterior make it seem uninspiring, this belies the fact that it could still "make the jump to light speed" and leverage incredible power if the right pilot is at the helm. In essence, the

Millennium Falcon is an authentic reflection of its owner, Han Solo, who has a rugged, rebellious exterior that conceals his genuine passion, bravery, and loyalty.

At this stage, I don't expect that you know what authenticity means when it comes to your verbal delivery. As we progress with practical guidance in this chapter, you'll want to think in terms of experimentation for gradual development and allow the process to inform you of what will work best *for you*. Some of the tips I provide will come naturally and may be incorporated into your repertoire right away. Others will feel wonky, which means that either you aren't ready to employ them, or they simply aren't right for you.

Discomfort is an obvious sign that something isn't working, but there are occasions when you are uncertain or simply can't tell. A practical way of measuring the success of your experimentation is to invite wise counsel (as discussed in Chapter Four) to provide feedback. While this might make you feel vulnerable and exposed, it's much better to get honest input during the experimentation phase before you hit the stage and risk coming across as unauthentic. Don't think of it as admitting weakness, but rather as a step in your continual growth; everyone can strive to do better.

You can also liken the process to shopping for new clothes. While trying on a new dress or jacket in a store, you might check yourself out in the mirror but still not have a clue if the garment looks good on you or not. What do you do? Ask the salesperson for an objective opinion, of course.

Below is the secret formula:

Authenticity + Counsel = Comfortable Progress

We will now progress further on your luminary journey, as I offer you practical counsel on the three main elements of nonverbal skills: vocal articulation, facial expression, and body movement.

Mic Check

If you happen to be listening to the audio version of this book, the spoken words are entering your ear canals as sound waves. Once they reach your eardrum, the vibrations pass from your middle ear bones into your inner ears. This snail-shaped area, known as the cochlea, has an average of 18,000 tiny hair cells that convert the vibrations into electrical signals and send them to your brain through your hearing nerve. Right now, your brain is telling you that you are hearing my voice describe how sound travels, and that audio resonance with your audience is crucial.

I'm sure there have been times when you were an audience member and became frustrated because the speaker's voice was too soft, too loud, or too garbled. Even in today's high-tech environments, there are still many occasions when the mic doesn't work right, or the volume is set at the wrong level. It's equally as possible that a speaker's voice isn't in sync with the technology and/or room acoustics.

Monotone Robot ←————————→ **Opera Singer**

The way we package our words when they come out of our mouths is crucial in terms of how people receive them. We should support our audience's ears by focusing on our voices, which in my opinion, is the most important element of presentation delivery. Many people I've trained notice the greatest shift in their public speaking effectiveness occurs when they adjust their pace, tone, and volume to improve the rate, inflection, and strength of their speech. My team has found that these modifications contribute to an average increase in public speaking confidence by over nine percent.

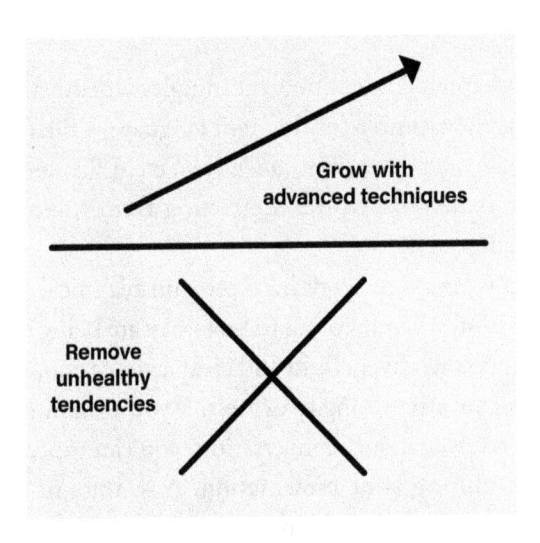

In the previous chapter, I offered a model for evaluating distracting tendencies, habits that fall below the line. Before we move on to more advanced techniques above the line, we'll start by identifying the three most detrimental pitfalls of vocalization that plague technical speakers and create a ceiling on their personal development:

1. Using filler words.

2. Speaking too quickly.

3. Sounding like a monotone robot.

To avoid these common pitfalls, we want to develop your precision, pace, and pitch. For each issue, I'll first clarify the problem with context. Then I'll provide practical solutions to not only remove the distracting tendencies (below the line), but also to replace them with more skillful alternatives for better overall vocalization (move above the line).

Precision

In the last chapter, I identified meaningless, distracting words that people use as they fumble for the right language—filler words, such as *um, like, kinda, sorta, you know, okay, well,* etc. Like weeds in a garden, they appear as invasive clutter, detracting from the magnificence of your messaging.

You and your teams work hard on your technical projects, which deserve precision when it comes to how they are being described. Your audience expects relatively fluid and clear articulation, so they can follow what you are attempting to express. If you are someone who uses a lot of filler words in casual conversation, you can expect that they will also crop up during your presentation. Any amount of nervousness will only exacerbate the problem.

To reduce unnecessary clutter from your vocabulary, start by identifying your weeds. Most speakers aren't even aware of their filler words because they have become second nature to them. While there isn't such a thing as an instantaneous "weed killer," there are a couple of things you can do right away: Record your speech and play it back while being on the lookout for filler words, and/or practice your presentation in front of someone in your trusted inner circle and specifically ask the question, "Did you catch any repetitive, unnecessary words, such as *like* or *um*?"

Once you have identified your pattern of filler words and heard how invasive they can be, your brain will become more alert to them and better detect when they are about to creep in. They become tagged as unwanted, enabling you to filter them out in your daily communication. The less you use them while away from the stage (or Zoom screen), the fewer times they will appear in your commentary.

The next step for reducing filler words is to shift attention away from them by focusing more on the specific words you want to use. Back in Chapter Six, I provided tactics on how to organize your talking points around succinct messages that accentuate your talking points with sound bites. If you concentrate on the key words in your presentation, you will reduce the risk of filler words popping up when you speak in front of an audience. This requires *practice*. Why? Because preparedness and confidence counter the need to fall back and rely on filler words.

> SIDECAR
>
> I'm not suggesting that you must memorize every word of your presentation in the form of a black-tie speech. Be aware, however, that the number of *ums* you spew is inversely proportional to the amount of familiarity you have with your talking points. Remember:
>
> *less familiarity = more filler*

If you doubt that practice is valuable, consider one of the most inspirational orators of all-time: Winston Churchill, Prime Minister of the United Kingdom during World War II. You may have heard bits and pieces of his speeches and/or have been educated about his public speaking prowess, but did you also know that he had a debilitating lisp? Some people who experience this challenge shrink from making such public speeches—but not Churchill. Instead, he worked even harder on his elocution, fine-tuning his speeches down to the last syllable. Churchill described his arduous preparation this way: "If you want me to speak for two minutes, it will take me three weeks of preparation…If you want me to speak for an hour, I am ready now."

My point in referencing Churchill is to emphasize the importance of making every word count and minimizing filler words that don't. Note that I specifically used the word "minimize" and not something stronger, such as "eliminate." Here's the rub: At the risk of negating everything I just advised about ditching filler words, there are some occasions when their usage at the right moments can reinforce authenticity. Many audiences see right through fake, over-rehearsed speakers who are so perfect they sound like political puppets. If an occasional *um* slips into your delivery, don't sweat it. Your audience might view you as more of a real person without pretenses, which could win them over.

We'll return to filler words in the next section, as I have another tip to share on the subject that falls under the category of pace.

Pace

I'm not a car guy. I don't even know how to drive a stick shift. One thing I do know, however, is in an automatic car, the gears shift up and down on their own, depending on the driver's speed.

Similarly, when it comes to speaking, we can leverage our pace to receive several communication benefits. The first is tied to the previous guidance about removing filler words. Once you build your awareness of them and practice, the single best way to reduce them is by working on the pace of speech. If you're speaking at the equivalent of seventy-five miles per hour, any filler words will jostle your audience around like unexpected speed bumps.

While auctioneers and sports commentators push the boundaries of what listeners can handle when they reach the neighborhood of 400 words per minute (wpm), the average conversational pace for speaking is 150 wpm. If you're someone who constantly pushes the pedal (of your tongue) to the metal (of your mouth), you are likely thrusting out 200 wpm. The problem here is that five to ten percent of those words are probably fillers. It might not seem like much, but one filler word per sentence could be enough to irritate an audience and cause them to tune out. My advice? Pump the breaks and slow down.

Another potential issue to recognize regarding your pacing is what I refer to as *flat speed*. If you speak at the same pace throughout, it comes across as predictable, which lulls your audience to sleep.

This begs the question: How do we decide when to speed up versus slow down?

Speed up when you...

- Present logical information that is easy to follow (i.e., general context).

- Try to build excitement in a story.

- Encourage urgency for a project and need people to respond ASAP.

- Offer content that will benefit from rapid delivery to build audience attention.

Slow down when you...

- Want to add variation to your standard fast speaking pace.

- Need to reduce filler words.

- Discuss serious or important topics.

- Hope technical content will land well by providing time for your audience to bite, chew, and digest it.

To conclude this section, I'm leaving you with one more suggestion. Before I do, however, I need to take a brief...

...*pause.*

Did you notice how your brain leaned in while processing the above break? A deliberate, well-timed break forces you to moderate your speed and give attendees a chance to catch up with you. The

> **SIDECAR**
>
> Establishing a *purposeful pace* will help align your cadence with your content. It allows you to infuse an enjoyable rhythm to earn and maintain your audience's attention.
>
> Remember: You are the expert, which means it's your responsibility to guide your audience who is following your lead. This is especially important because audience members typically remember only ten to thirty percent of what they hear in presentations. If you want people to retain your key messages, occasionally slow down and articulate your messages as clearly as possible.

momentary silence—accompanied by a relaxed but unmoving posture—can be powerful for audience engagement. Listeners will sit up at attention wondering why you broke from your script. They think: *What's happening? Why did he stop talking? He must have something crucial to say.*

This technique will pay dividends in terms of increasing your audience's attention span while conveying to them that you have enough confidence to pause. At the same time, the conscious break prevents you from adding filler words because your brain has more time to deliver precise words to your mouth.

Pitch

My usage of the word *pitch* has nothing to do with baseball or a sales call. Instead, it refers to *tone* and *volume*. Whereas pace concerns the rate of speech, tone reflects the measurement of how and when your voice goes up and down. Your tone can serve as a useful tool to emphasize key points, especially when you want to land memorable sound bites. The right modulation helps prevent you from sounding too monotone or robotic. You are looking to speak in a conversational tone that is pleasant, inviting, and engaging.

Tone can sometimes confuse people. A simple way to make it more concrete is to take a page from written communication and think about it in terms of punctuation marks. The comma, period, and question mark can become your friends. A comma can serve as a half break (or half pause) to separate distinguishable parts of a sentence. A period may be viewed as a full stop (complete pause), enabling you to take a slightly longer break and shift the sound of your voice. A question mark means you are raising your voice an octave to address the audience directly; this means an extra pause afterwards to solicit the desired audience response. Sprinkling your presentation with audience questions gives you an opportunity to vary your tone while appealing to your audience's innate curiosity.

Punctuation can be taken a few steps further by thinking in terms of somewhat longer breaks, such as the start of the next paragraph or introduction of a section with a new heading. For an even more radical transition—such as a complete change in subject or theme—you can pause even longer as if to indicate the equivalent of a next chapter. You want to do this sparingly, as too many lengthy pauses can feel draggy and/or disruptive. The main consideration is mixing things up enough to always keep your presentation lively and interesting, saving the pauses for when they are truly needed and can have the greatest impact.

"*Wait a minute, Jack!*" I hear you exclaim. "*I thought you were also going to talk about volume!*"

Did I pique your curiosity by imagining your voice as a reader speaking exclamatory sentences (with exclamation points)? That is one way to signal to yourself to raise the volume of your voice. You can accomplish the same thing by bolding or italicizing certain words or phrases in your talking points that require emphasis and slightly higher volume.

When you are drafting your talking points in the notes section of your slides—no more than five concise bullets that each fit on one line—bold one to two key words per point. Don't worry about memorizing the bullets, but rather, practice them to develop enough familiarity so that you can remember to add vocal emphasis and adjust your precision, pace, and pitch on the bolded words to further impress them in the ears and on the brains of your listeners.

Note that you only want your volume to go one notch above your comfort zone; otherwise, it might come across as shouting. Most people hover around sixty decibels in conversations. On a scale of one to ten, if you typically speak at a level of six, I encourage you to try seven on for size and notice your audience's reaction. Known as "reading the room," this involves monitoring and adjusting your delivery based on the body language and facial expressions of attendees. (Hint: If they're looking down, you should move on to the next topic or be bold and ask them if they have any questions or need additional information.)

If you're unsure about your volume level and speaking in a conference room, try speaking to the person furthest away from you. If you're on stage, keep your volume strong because the audio technician can always balance your levels. This also helps release nervous energy that tends to get trapped in your sternum.

Speakers who have a flat, dronelike voice are difficult to follow for long periods of time. It can become boring within the first couple of minutes. For this reason, I recommend a *dynamic*—but not dramatic—tone because you risk sounding forced and arrogant, which can put off an audience.

As mentioned earlier, your goal is to improve your delivery mechanics while remaining authentic. Han Solo serves as a good model for this. While he occasionally crosses the line into cockiness for Hollywood appeal, he doesn't concern himself about what others think about him. When it comes to varying your pitch with more tonality, just make sure to avoid flat speech by occasionally adding some vocal inflection.

Look Like You Care

We will now expand beyond our mouths to our eyes and the rest of our face for more deliberate delivery techniques: proper eye contact and facial expression. In the last chapter, I shared a powerful tip about focusing on people's foreheads instead of looking into their eyes, which can feel intimidating. Another suggestion is to concentrate on the eyes of one or two friendly, familiar faces in the audience.

Be careful about trying to engage too many pairs of eyes, as this can come across as *scanning*. Imagine your head resembling a lawn sprinkler head showering the audience with jittery looks from left to right and back again.

Another common mistake to avoid is allowing your eyeballs to wander aimlessly around the room. This tendency is often paired with a glass of filler words as we ponder the cosmos by staring up at the… *um, like, kinda*…ceiling or speak to the…*uh, so, sorta*…floor.

That said, looking down can be a useful technique when it's deliberate and combined with a pause. If you've spoken for a while and imparted a massive amount of information, your audience will completely understand if you take a breath and gather your thoughts. When you lift your head back up and look at the audience, you send a signal that you are refreshed and ready to re-engage with additional valuable content. At the same time, you are building anticipation for what's coming next. Be patient as you practice this: The technique can take a while to master, as it's easy to default to scanning and/or blurting out filler words when you raise your head.

You're on Mute

I'm sure you already know firsthand that many presentation scenarios have shifted to video conferencing methods, such as Zoom. The fact that your image and voice are appearing on laptop, desktop, or even phone screens doesn't mean you can take anything for granted, especially that your mic is on. The following tips are second nature for many but important reminders to check, especially if you're presenting virtually.

First, if you aren't up to date with the latest video conferencing technology, do some prep work in advance. For example, Zoom requires periodic updates that might involve restarting your computer. If you are presenting on this platform, you want to be sure you have the latest version so you aren't struggling to restart and re-log into the site, which can make you late to join your own meeting. You'll also want to brush up on how to send messages to others (especially private ones that only one or a few people can see), record a meeting, share your screen, and make a participant a cohost.

Here are a few more friendly reminders that most readers know by now but may be helpful for you who are less versed with virtual presentations. The first is ensuring to the best of your ability that you are in a setting with a strong Wi-Fi connection. There is nothing worse for attendees than suffering through frozen screens, especially since they happen during the most inopportune times (such as midsentence or when you are making a weird expression). The next issue is about sound: Be certain that this setting on your computer and any external mics are turned up to a strong volume ahead of time.

Whether you are presenting from your normal workspace or somewhere else, make certain that the background is clean, organized, and professional. To reduce the issue the background noise heard from your side of the call, try headphones and any noise cancellation features in your video conferencing software.

Audio is just one thing that can potentially disrupt video calls. If you are working from home during an important presentation, take extra special care to prevent roommates, partners, children, and pets from bombing your video. Although they can sometimes be a fun distraction, they can also come across as disruptive and unprofessional in certain settings. Pets can be cute but a dog constantly barking on a Zoom might ruin a presentation.

You always want to have good lighting but without any sun glare. The camera lens should be positioned at eye level to avoid seeming as if you are looking up or down and to capture your upper face and body. At all costs, resist the temptation to look at yourself in the selfie window, as this causes you to have poor eye contact with the camera and thus the people watching you. If you have slides and/or notes, I recommend moving the window displaying them just below the camera, so your eyes remain focused in the right position.

You shouldn't have your eyes locked on the camera the entire time, however, as you still need to seem as if you are live, authentic, and engaged with the attendees. When speaking to a larger group (more than three people), every few minutes you can progressively move clockwise from one audience member to then next before working back. Try to avoid talking to your slides, instead of your virtual audience members, as you will come across as reading rather than speaking.

---- SIDECAR ----

I would never tell you to smile just for the sake of it. In fact, some experts recommend against it as a rule. My professional take on this is that people like to see a smiling face every now and then to lighten the mood of a presentation, avoid coming across as too stoic or serious, and help people feel at ease. You can also smile to signal when you have positive news to share with the group.

Face Time

According to an article from Michigan State University, it takes forty-seven facial muscles to frown and only thirteen to smile. Hopefully, you aren't going to do much of the former during a presentation, but I do encourage the latter occasionally—especially in the beginning of your talk—to convey a friendly, welcoming appearance. You don't want to smile too widely or too often, as this can come across as fake or unintentionally smug.

The Anatomy of Body Language
If you'll recall from the last chapter, fifty-five percent of our communication can be determined by body language. This means you can have informative content, brilliant slides, and excellent oration skills but still give an ineffective presentation. Body language is vital, and I've broken it down into three key elements, with best practices for each included below: hand gestures, posture, and movement.

What Do I Do with My Hands?
One of the most common questions that comes up during speaker rehearsals is around the use of hands. When executed with the right restraint, timely hand gestures not only express your thoughts, but also convey your enthusiasm for the topic. According to body language expert Dr. Carol Kinsey Goman, "Gesturing can help people form clearer thoughts, speak in tighter sentences, and use more declarative language."

As always, try to remain authentic while being purposeful with the use of your hands to help deliver key messages that match your tone and rhythm. In other words, fire a few engaging shots with hand gestures and then put them back in their holsters. By this, I mean arms at their sides with elbows raised ninety degrees and palms up in front of your waist, which comes across as welcoming and inclusive. If you happen to be seated, rest your hands on the table or on your lap until you decide to strategically emphasize key messages. If you're like me and tend to get carried away when you are passionate about a topic, be mindful of excessive gesturing that can come across as air traffic control and distract your audience. If you're on the other side of the spectrum and relatively reserved with your body language, try to bring your hands up and out one time per slide to add a bit more enthusiasm to your talk while remaining comfortably composed.

Practical Posture

If you are seated during a presentation, always remember what moms told us when we were eating around the dinner table: *Sit up straight!*

Good posture—whether you are sitting or standing—involves keeping your spine upright and tall with your shoulders back, which opens your diaphragm for stronger enunciation. Your feet should be shoulder width apart to create a confident pose that is also comfortable and demonstrates a grounded demeanor. This posture is not only better for your back, but it also prevents giving a closed off, slouchy impression.

If you're presenting in a conference room with more than five people in attendance, consider standing up. It improves your command of the room and reduces nervous energy. Some casual work cultures are uneasy with this arrangement. If this is the case for you, consider asking the room upfront if it's okay to stand while presenting because you're so excited to share your update that you can't sit still!

Another tip for when you're speaking to a group in a conference room is around using a whiteboard. Whether you're sketching a workflow diagram or working out a tough math problem, make sure to keep the room engaged as you use the board. Avoid turning your back on the audience or speaking toward the board too much, as this can hinder engagement. Instead, while writing on the board, turn your body three quarters toward the audience and speak a bit louder to ensure you retain everyone's attention.

Whether standing in a conference room or sitting in a Zoom meeting, remember to up-level your presence when presenting with a strong upright posture to demonstrate a more professional look than if you were simply attending a meeting.

Methodical Movement

When it comes to positioning yourself and moving around in front of in-person audiences, there are a few important considerations to maximize your spacing. If you are presenting on a stage to a larger group, the general rule of thumb is to position yourself in the center, a couple of feet from the edge. If there isn't a stage but you're presenting in a larger conference room, a lectern or podium can be fine, but it may also create a barrier to connecting with your audience, so try to step away from it at various points. You want to be at a good angle that allows you to view the projection screens or monitors without blocking them.

Depending on your personal style, you're likely going to be standing still for much—but hopefully not all—of your presentation, so consider adding some intentional movement. Some well-timed steps can liven things up and add energy to the room. You never want to get carried away and pace back and forth across the stage, however, as this will make you seem anxious. I recommend no more than three points—left, right, and center, so you can step forward when delivering key messages—to allow dynamic engagement while maintaining your composure. If you don't feel comfortable doing this, plant your feet and hold your ground while considering the best practices we discussed about posture.

To stay above the line and prevent distracting tendencies, avoid all swaying, rocking, shaking, twisting, stretching, jerking, or dancing. Occasional and light shifting of your weight from one side to the other is okay but stay mindful if you have a habit of doing the cha-cha!

What Else?

My team and I have spent thousands of hours training professionals on public speaking. Having noticed that the same questions always seem to pop up, I'll end this chapter by addressing them head-on in the following section.

1. Q: *What about slides?*
   A: What about them? My apologies. I admit I am being

a bit snarky here because I see too many speakers hide behind their presentation decks, which detracts from their presence. Slides should only be regarded as *visual aids* to support the delivery of your content. They shouldn't be considered the main focus. Audience members may benefit from and enjoy some visuals, but they much prefer to connect with human beings.

There isn't a "magic number" of slides but less is more. A rule of thumb is one minute per slide, which varies upon your personal speech pattern and the amount of content you must impart. If you are speaking for thirty minutes, err on the side of fewer slides (around twenty) so you don't run out of time or overwhelm your audience while also allowing a few minutes at the end for Q&A.

In terms of slide design, you don't need to create something revolutionary. It needs to supplement and accentuate your verbal presentation, not outdo or overwhelm it. A simple, clear, and professional look often works best. The good news is that you don't have to reinvent the wheel. You can emulate a slide design you like or ask your in-house creative design team for a basic template to build on. Once again, I recommend you read Nancy Duarte's excellent book *Resonate* for more detailed instruction on design.

With my disclaimers out of the way, I'll get off my anti-slide soapbox and provide a few quick tips on creating an effective slide deck:

- Write clear, succinct, catchy headers that capture the main message of the slide.

- Use subheadings if they add contextual value to

the header and don't distract from the slide's main message.

- Feature less text and more visually stimulating graphics and images.

- Incorporate uncomplicated images, such as diagrams, workflows, graphs, or screenshots of digital applications for technical presentations.

- If you don't have enough images, depict key messages with icons.

- Integrate a text-based slide between every few visual slides to make them more dynamic and less predictable.

- Include no more than three bullets on a text-based slide.

- Navigate your audience's eyes with colored indicators—red circles or green arrows—as you explain graphs, photos, workflows, diagrams, etc.

- Ensure consistent font size, shape, and color of all words on a slide.

- Consider subtle coloring in the background of slides to accentuate but not clash with images and text.

- Insert one or two inspirational or humorous graphics (i.e. memes) to keep things light and interesting as long as it's appropriate for your audience and objectives.

- Show brief videos or GIFs where appropriate to liven things up.

- Leverage animations to break up key elements of your explanations so you can progressively reveal them as you speak to them, but avoid overly dramatic builds that distract from the messages.

2. Q: *How do I look like a TED speaker?*
A: Don't do this! *Talk Like TED,* by Carmine Gallo, is a fantastic book filled with useful heuristics. However, while TED speakers generally have intriguing content to share, most of them come across to me as over coached and over polished. This is precisely why I started this chapter with comments about authenticity. Some trainers push stuffy suit-and-tie delivery mechanics that diminish audience trust, so I encourage you to aim for a more conversational style.

3. Q: *How do I elicit positive responses from my audience?*
A: Always exude positivity. In a joint study at the University of Minnesota and Michigan State, researchers Joyce E. Bono and Remus Ilies discovered that subjects who rate high in upbeat charisma tend to invoke more favorable emotions from written and spoken communication than those on the low end. Their passionate approach drives engagement and increases their ability to persuade audiences. With that said, avoid sounding like an infomercial

salesperson by balancing upbeat confidence with grounded composure, so you keep your delivery natural.

4. Q: *How do I avoid passing out when I speak to large groups?*
A: Public speaking is scary! It's normal to feel anxious and nervous when presenting. Some people get so stricken by fear that they lose their train of thought, freeze, or even have panic attacks.

How do you curb fear? *Preparation.* You want to think of yourself like a professional athlete preparing for a big game. Their secret? Visualization: Every day, they imagine themselves performing their athletic activity to perfection. It's possible to convert mental energy into physical prowess to improve their focus and manifest success. Star baseball, football, and basketball players do this, as well as Olympic tennis stars and swimmers. A study orchestrated at the Olympic Training Center in Colorado Springs, CO found that one hundred percent of coaches and ninety-seven percent of athletes supported usage of visualization techniques to enhance their performance. If it works for them, it can work for you!

In the days leading up to your presentation, spend a few minutes in the morning and/or afternoon imagining the setting of your presentation with you delivering it well. When visualizing your presentation, sit in a comfortable position, close your eyes, and breathe in and out a few times. Each breath should be slow and deliberate; it's not a race and you want to feel relaxed. Once you are in a good mental and physical state, visualize yourself delivering your presentation. Imagine walking into a room full of engaged people who appreciate all the work you put into preparing to speak with them. Roll the entire experience like a movie scene: You can hear your confident voice, see your strong posture, and feel the excited applause from attendees at the end of your talk.

The key to a successful visualization is to play the scene the same way each time with you achieving your desired success by the end. This way, when the big moment arrives, you'll perform just as you did in your mind's eye, just like a professional athlete hitting the game-winning shot.

The other half of preparation involves *memorization*. I'm not suggesting you learn everything word-for-word, especially since this could hinder your authenticity. However, I do think it's a smart idea to "memorize" the first thirty seconds of your talk, meaning that you know eighty to ninety percent of your opening comments, since the hardest part of public speaking is the beginning. Committing your first few lines to memory will ease your nervous system before you start while also supporting strong articulation with minimal filler words out of the gate.

I also advise you "warm up your engine" prior to flooring the gas pedal. You don't want to walk up in silence and "cold start" by abruptly jumping right into your comments, as you wouldn't be giving your brain and body a chance to adapt to the environment. Rather than a cold start, take deep breaths ahead of time to clear your head. While approaching the stage (or front of the conference room), recite the opening lines to yourself. As you walk up to your speaking spot (or turn on your Zoom video), take another deep breath and calmly ease into your opening exactly as you did in your visualization.

Takeaways

- Start your presentation with the empowerment promise, a statement of what you vow to deliver by the time you are done.

- To convey authenticity, speak with authority about what you know from your unique viewpoint and avoid anything that might sacrifice your personal integrity.

- Avoid using filler words, speaking too quickly, and sounding like a monotone robot.

- Practice precision, pace, and pitch.

- Ensure your technical setup—such as your mic and slide deck—are all functioning properly ahead of time.

- Establish the right body language in front of an audience, which means using your hands and movement purposefully while maintaining eye contact with the audience.

- Remember that slides are valuable and should look relatively professional but are secondary to stage presence, body language, verbalization, and spoken content.

- Visualize your presentation in advance and "memorize" your opening lines to start strong and allow yourself to settle in.

- Check out Professor Winston's famous video for more presentation heuristics: https://www.youtube.com/watch?v=Unzc731iCUY

FINAL ACT

Closing Comments—The End

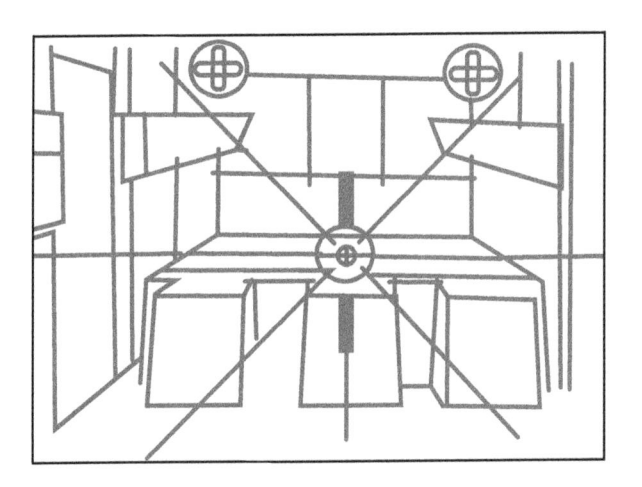

CHAPTER NINE

Time Well Spent

Congratulations—you've made it through the luminary gauntlet! We've covered a lot of ground about empathetic effectiveness, crafted content, and deliberate delivery. Before I unleash you to continue your journey for ongoing development, I will wrap things up with final takeaways, reveal how to handle audience Q&A (question and answer); and provide some insights around EQ (emotional intelligence) to help you shine even brighter with your technical storytelling.

Before sharing the takeaways, I encourage you to always remember: *Development work is a journey.* Any self-help scheme that promises immediate results overnight is probably one that needs some help itself. Like plants, humans need ongoing nourishment to continue our slow growth over a lengthy period. I hope this book has been an enjoyable and practical source of nourishment for the short-term while also deepening and strengthening your roots for growth that will be sustained for many seasons to come.

Top-line Takeaways

In case you haven't noticed by now, I've been presenting this book—an instructional guide on how to develop and deliver technical presentations—in the form of an exemplary talk to model what I've been teaching. The outline of the talk was based on the framework of breaking a story into the three main components we discussed in Chapter Six: a beginning; a middle; and an end. To simplify this story structure, I mentioned a quote early on, "Tell them what you are going to tell them, tell them, then tell them what you told them." In line with this approach, I began our journey in the Introduction by "telling you" what was to come while also hooking your attention with compelling research about first impressions and an Empowerment Promise of what you would expect to gain by the end of the book.

After setting the stage in the beginning, I guided you through the middle section of this book, which was structured into three main sub-sections based on the rule of three to keep the main messages organized and digestible. If I hadn't set the stage with a proper intro and instead dove right into a bunch of technical explanations without ample context, you would probably have been overwhelmed and buried this book on a shelf. Rather, I used the three sub-sections of the middle to present the breadth and depth of our work together that represent the luminary journey in the form of a sequential workflow connecting the main components of a presentation:

> Empathetic Effectiveness (who & why) >
> Crafted Content (what) > Deliberate Delivery (how)

Now that I've closed by "telling you what I told you" with those takeaways, we'll head into the finale with insights about how to best handle audience questions before wrapping up with some intriguing guidance about executive presence.

Discussion Leadership

Whether planned or unplanned, answering questions can be challenging, especially with technical audiences who are often brilliant and critical. All your great work to analyze your audience, orient around objectives, craft content, and confidently deliver your presentation will be wasted if your hungry audience devours you with intimidating questions. You can try to hold off questions until the end of your talk, but in my experience—especially with senior leaders in attendance—the questioning comes much sooner. When you least expect it—often in the middle of your presentation while you are concentrating on driving home a crucial point—someone in the audience raises a hand (if they're polite) and lobs a curveball at you, interrupting your train of thought and perhaps disturbing the other attendees.

This may feel like a distraction, if not an all-out annoyance, but here's the uncomfortable truth: You *want* your audience to ask questions because it enables more discussion, which could lead to more interest in your work. You can't assume that the audience understands everything you have been saying or that you provided every ounce of

---

SIDECAR

There are some selfish presenters who spend an entire session diving deep into their dense decks without pausing to allow themselves or their audiences to come up for a breath of air. When they do so, they miss the opportunity to solicit comments, which would have been greatly appreciated by the attendees.

Remember: Audience members are the protagonists of your story. If you ignore them, you aren't fulfilling your role as a wise guide and risk leaving them in the dark without all the necessary information needed to support your efforts.

more discussion = *more engagement*

information they require. In addition to helping your audience follow your talk and support your work, additional dialogue in the form of Q&A can also help you demonstrate more credibility and earn the audience's trust through transparent discussion leadership.

The secrets to navigating questions start with allocating an appropriate amount of time for them. If you tell your audience to hold all questions until the end of your presentation, you better keep to your promise, or some people will be leaving the room upset that you stole the show with too many slides. Most presenters say they'll reserve a few minutes at the end for Q&A, but this tends to fail because they don't plan things out well enough and run out of time.

So, how much time should you carve out? Unless you are explicitly told to present for the entire session without allowing questions, I suggest an ambitious goal of allocating *one-third* of your total time for discussion. If you are granted fifteen minutes to provide an update at an All Hands meeting, break it down to ten minutes of content and five for Q&A. For a lengthier forty-five-minute talk at a tech conference, leave fifteen minutes at the end for questions.

SIDECAR

Tracking time should be simple, but it's often overlooked. To avoid constantly running out of time or ending your presentations too early, make sure you have visual access to a timer. If you're presenting on stage, ask for a countdown clock to be placed next to the confidence monitors, so you can frequently check on your progress. If you're speaking at a virtual engagement, pull up the timer app on your phone and set it near your laptop to ensure proper pacing. No matter where you are in your content, when you have two minutes left on the timer, start transitioning to your closing lines, so you land the plane smoothly without appearing rushed.

The homestretch of technical presentations is an opportune moment to finish strong as you move from your content to questions while being mindful of your energy level. Transitioning from your presentation can be tricky, especially after you've been on a roll speaking for so long. At this point, you risk exhaustion and overheating, which can diminish your cognitive strength for questions. To prevent this, I recommend that you pause to take a drink of water followed by a deep breath to show up as your best self, especially if you need to handle a controversial discussion.

Composure is key because some questioners can be snarky and/or try to undermine your presentation. On other occasions, someone might innocently ask something that you simply can't answer at that moment. While either motivation is entirely possible—people can have all kinds of agendas—you don't want to reveal shakiness, as this can be interpreted as incompetent. You also don't want to counter in an obnoxious tone—even if it matches that of the audience member—as it will come across as immature and potentially vindictive. You always want to be professional and take the high road.

Here are some practical steps that will help you best navigate audience questions:

1. *Acknowledge politely*
    - Instead of jumping the gun and reacting too hastily, buy yourself some time so you can respond more thoughtfully.

    - To buy some time, politely acknowledge the question with an initial comment, such as:

        a. *Thanks for bringing up the point, it's an important one about…*
        b. *Good question…*

c. *I appreciate you noticing that part of the project…*

- After the initial acknowledgement, state the questioner's name. Most people enjoy hearing their names aloud, so you'll win some points prior to proceeding to the next step.

    o For example, "Thanks for following up on that technical point, Alice."

2. *Paraphrase actively*
    - Use your active listening skills (covered in Chapter Two) by playing back key comments from questioners to ensure you heard the question correctly and understand what is being asked. Sometimes audience members pose questions that are embedded in monologues and contain lots of fluff, so it can be difficult to discern what they really want from you. An additional benefit of active listening is that it demonstrates to audience members that you are paying attention and care about their interests.

    - Active listening also helps you buy even *more* time for yourself because you are paraphrasing the question back to the questioner.

    - Below are some active listening prompts:

        o To play that back, it sounds like you're asking about part of the infra stack, is that right?

- Are you asking about the code I mentioned in my deep dive?
- I appreciate the extra context with your question—can you please clarify which part of the talk you are referring to?

3. *Respond intentionally*
   - Once you've bought some time to understand and process the question, you'll be better prepared to provide a thoughtful response.

   - Wherever possible, your comments should tie back to the objectives you set out for the talk, as this will improve the overall effectiveness of your content and drive additional retention of your key messages.

   - If answering the question won't help achieve your objectives and/or risks derailing the Q&A session, politely ask the questioner if you can follow up offline or at least place the question in the "parking lot" to be answered later, if there's time.

   - After you've responded to a question, ask the questioner whether your answer was sufficient. This is especially important if this individual happens to be a decision maker with the power to influence your work.

   - If you are pressed for time, transition from your answer to the next question, so you can control the dialogue and stay within your allotted time.

Below are a few examples of how the Q&A dialogue should flow based on the previously cited best practices:

Reader 1: Jack, what do I do if someone interrupts me mid-presentation before the Q&A session?

Jack: Good question, Reader 1, I appreciate you bringing up this important topic [politely acknowledge]. Interruptions are common, especially from senior leaders. To help me give you the most accurate answer: Are you asking me how to answer a question that comes up in the middle of your talk [active listening]?

Reader 1: Well, not exactly. I'd rather not answer questions in the middle of my presentation because they usually send my presentation down a rabbit hole, and then I don't have enough time to finish my slides.

Jack: Okay, I understand, thank you for clarifying. I hear you—it's really frustrating when people derail our presentations. My suggestion would be to consider your audience and objectives to help determine how to field questions that come up during your presentation time. If your audience consists of senior leaders and your objective is to gain their buy-in on the next phase of your project, then I would briefly address their questions as they come up. Let them know you'll elaborate on these points in greater detail later in the talk or at the end, so they feel heard.

Let's also consider a different scenario. Suppose your audience is made of peers and your objective is to fill them in on a new feature that you're rolling out, so you need to cover a lot of details and stay on track. If this is the case, you could politely tell attendees to hold mid-presentation questions until the Q&A at the end when you'll be happy to address them [*respond succinctly*].

Reader 2: Jack, how do I avoid "fluffy" presentations?

Jack: Thank you for the bold question, Reader 2. It sounds like you struggle with the core substance of your talks—but can you share more about what you mean by "fluffy"?

Reader 2: I'm actually good with crafting my core content; it's more about presenting with integrity. I see so many senior leaders talk a lot on stage, but they don't follow through. They wave their hands about big ideas and then have little to show for it.

Jack: Got it. Thank you for clarifying. This sensitive topic resonates with me. Personally, I can't stand "talking with no walking" and plan to address the topic at the end of this chapter.

Emotional Intelligence (EQ)

The expression Emotional Intelligence (EQ) was originated by Peter Salovey and John D. Mayer in 1990. Daniel Goleman was intrigued by their research and in 1995 built on it in his masterwork *Emotional Intelligence*. Since then, EQ has been adopted by myriad corporate coaches, executives, and HR professionals to increase holistic leadership competence by balancing intellectual brilliance and emotional composure. For our purposes, we are only going to cover the core elements of EQ:

1. Knowing one's emotions: self-awareness with recognition of feelings.

2. Managing emotions: handling emotions so they are appropriate.

3. Motivating oneself: marshaling emotions to serve a goal.

4. Recognizing emotions in others: having empathy for people.

5. Handling relationships: demonstrating competence in social interactions.

You may be wondering: *What does EQ have to do with technical storytelling?*

Let's go back to the three-step approach to answering questions I provided earlier in the chapter. Note that I specifically chose the word *respond* because it is tied to a critical distinction regarding EQ. Answering questions about our work—especially pointed ones—can be intimidating. When we are in the spotlight and all eyes are on us, the slightest question can feel threatening. *Is he suggesting that I've made a mistake? Is she trying to embarrass me? Does he want to show me up to make himself seem smarter?*

An audience member with a tough question may or may not be attacking your knowledge or authority on a subject, but either way, the result on your psyche might be the same: Your nervous system goes on high alert. Your heart thumps, your pulse soars, you perspire profusely, and your mind gets clouded with worry. While experiencing fight-or-flight response, your first *reaction* is for the "cave brain" to go on the attack and start lashing. This is the *worst* way to deal with a challenging question, as your tone and words might come across as defensive, argumentative, and unsure of your work. Instead of controlling your presence, you suddenly seem weak and have something to hide. This is why EQ and managing your emotions are so vital in these situations.

Responding is quite different from *reacting*. The latter—which is triggered by fight-or-flight—means we'll spit out unthoughtful answers that make us appear frazzled. By contrast, when we buy ourselves time with the methodical approach explained above, it enables us to move beyond a knee-jerk reaction, so we can respond calmly and with clarity. More time allows us to pause, relax, think, distill our thoughts, and articulate well-prepared comments. When we respond by tapping into our emotional intelligence, we adeptly manage what's going on *inside* ourselves to better convey composure on the *outside*.

There is another reason why I conclude my instruction with this brief overview of EQ. As I've hopefully made clear throughout this book, effective communication is the key to developing strong relationships while conveying the significance of your work. If you have purported yourself with high EQ throughout your presentation and sustained it until the end of an intense Q&A, you will have delivered your messages and garnered support for your ideas and projects. You will also have educated people, earned their trust, and built a powerful foundation for your career. The secret?

Better communication = better trajectory

Now What?

Words have the power to change the world. While there is some conflicting research on the matter, most studies have formed the conclusion that adults utter an average of 16,000 words per day. On the flip side, the average person hears *20,000-30,000* words per day. This suggests that we verbally communicate about 1,000 words per hour that can potentially impact other people's lives.

We've been identifying oral communication as a primary factor in working with people and influencing the world around us. However, it's just *one* factor—not *the* factor. As powerful as words are—especially when they're presented in conjunction with effective storytelling—they're mostly *the means*. While there are instances when speeches and friendly conversation are *the ends* in themselves because we enjoy connection through communication, talk alone won't cut it. If all we did was babble in our professional and personal lives, nothing would ever get done. *Action* represents the second half of the equation.

As we wind down our journey with closing guidance, I encourage you to consider a message that answers Reader 2's question about avoiding fluffy presentations: *Walk it out*. Don't be the hand waving fluff ball who sounds nice but lacks integrity. If I've filled your head with some nice-sounding ideas about storytelling but they don't sink in and translate into productivity and growth, I will have failed. I can speak with authority on this topic because I've been guilty of it myself. I've neglected to walk out my words on more than one occasion. I look back on some moments of my early career and cringe because of how arrogant and empty I must have seemed when I talked up a storm but subsequently didn't follow through on my commitments.

You owe it to yourself and your career to shine with integrity and inspire others to do the same by *walking out* the learnings of this book. The message about authenticity conveyed in Chapter Eight will only serve you if you also embrace *accountability*. Avoid turning into a talking head who spews out eloquent speeches that are full of hot air. Time is precious; don't waste it with empty words.

Journey of a Thousand Presentations

All right, it's time for me to step off my anti-hypocrisy soap box and concede that, out of all the learnings provided in this book, *walking it out* might seem the most overwhelming. Working on any new skill—especially related to the world's number one fear, public speaking—is intimidating. To alleviate the intimidation, consider luminary and founder of Taoism, Lao Tzu, who famously pronounced, "A journey of a thousand miles begins with a single step."

My final words of encouragement to support your ongoing journey: *Take* it *one presentation at a time*. I know it sounds cliche but, in this instance, I must reiterate that public speaking is all about *progressive development*. Incremental growth comes from experimenting with one new skill at a time until you master it and start to implement it naturally before you move on to the next one. This might involve spending a few extra minutes analyzing your audience prior to presenting at an upcoming meeting. Perhaps it might require being hyper focused on a specific objective embedded in your next tech conference talk. Or it might mean that you focus on the rule of three or reduce filler words in your next update to your leadership team.

Wherever you are in your luminary journey, stay hungry and humble. Complacency is the enemy of growth. Remember that we're all students of ourselves as we continue to learn with daily progress toward long-term illumination. As you walk it out one presentation at a time, "May the Force be with you."

Takeaways

- Build engagement by proactively planning for questions.

- Carve out one-third of your presentation time for Q&A.

- To field a challenging question, buy time by acknowledging politely, paraphrasing actively, and responding intentionally.

- Strengthen your emotional intelligence (EQ) by *responding* rather than *reacting*.

- Actions speak louder than words, so ensure that you *walk it out* after your presentation and take the action steps you promised to your audience.

- Continue your luminary journey one presentation and one skill at a time.

CHAPTER TEN

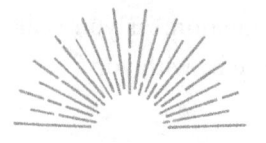

One Last Story

In the Introduction, I briefly mentioned a perilous trip I took while I was in Haiti that significantly changed the trajectory of my life. I hope the opening "teaser" grabbed your attention and you've been looking forward to hearing the full story of the adventure. I'm excited to now conclude this book *looping back* to my trip and offering an invitation to join the adventure.

It was on a hot and humid day in January 2016 that my friend and I found ourselves on a terrifying eight-hour bus ride from Santo Domingo in the Dominican Republic to Port Au Prince (PAP), Haiti. We thought the most frightening part would be the border check, where kids begged for money outside a rundown portable building guarded by men in old military outfits who carried rusty AK-47s. Presenting our passports for inspection turned out to be a breeze compared to what was about to come.

The next bump on our sketchy journey through the dilapidated shanty towns of Eastern Haiti occurred when we were pulled over by individuals who looked like police officers. We didn't know what words they exchanged with our bus driver, but they seemed heated until the driver apparently paid them off, so we could continue. We rolled through the dusty dirt roads for hours until we finally arrived at a rundown gas station in PAP, where chickens anxiously clucked around, and a gas station attendant with an old shotgun glared at us while we waited for our contacts to pick us up.

As the blazing sun began to set, we realized we had to face another obstacle caused by an error in our planning. We had miscalculated the difference in time zones, which meant that we gave our Haitian contacts the wrong arrival time and we didn't have cell service to let them know. Ordinarily, we would have been fine waiting longer than expected once we arrived in PAP; however, on the bus ride, we had a conversation with the only other two Caucasians who warned us that it was a bad time to be in the capital—especially at night—because protests had been stirred up by corrupt political elections.

The warning had us worried, but thankfully we avoided the riots and survived our eerie pitstop before we continued to the next leg of our adventure. Our contacts eventually arrived at the gas station, and we hopped in their rugged Land Cruiser for another eye-opening excursion for over five hours across the desolate mountains of Haiti. We were relieved when we finally arrived at our destination in the beautiful rural countryside, where we were joyfully greeted by some of the most hospitable and humble leaders I've ever met. They welcomed us with open arms, as they've done on each of my subsequent trips to Haiti where I happened to officially launch this book during my ninth visit. Every trip since the first has been an adventure, but I wouldn't have made it past the scary initial visit if it hadn't been for those inspiring leaders who illuminated what it means to live by faith.

Next-Level Luminaries

My story pales in comparison with that of our Haitian contacts—husband and wife Kristie and JeanJean Mompremier—who are now my dear friends and have impacted the lives of thousands of people for over two decades since they started serving in Haiti. In 2005, after completing his university studies in the United States, JeanJean and Kristie, who was from Iowa, returned to his Haitian hometown, Caïman, even though he had been exposed to unimaginable evil there during his childhood. Not only did his family live in squalor, but he roomed with his two brothers and cousin on their own in a six-by-six-foot space and had to trudge five hours to school with minimal access to bare necessities. To top off his heart-wrenching upbringing, JeanJean witnessed the murder of his father by a witchdoctor.

The Mompremiers could have avoided the dire circumstances of JeanJean's past and raised their two young daughters in the United States with a comfortable lifestyle, but they felt a calling to return to Haiti and decided to settle in Caïman. After cooking meals on an open fire outside their house, the couple would walk the streets in anguish as they watched impoverished children who were so hungry that they scavenged around fire pits to consume plates of ash.

One day, the grim site of kids' faces covered in ash and their bellies ballooning out from malnutrition become unbearable for the Mompremiers. Although they had precious little money, they initiated a feeding program for the local kids. Eventually, it blossomed into a fully staffed nonprofit organization which to this day continues to spread love to the Caïman community and beyond by teaching, equipping, and uniting local leaders. Among many other local-led programs, it now boasts nine nutrition centers, preschool through high schools, a health clinic, and an accredited university. The university has graduated 3,000+ students with degrees in medicine, theology, agriculture, and other areas to build up the next generation of Haitian leaders.

One of my personal favorite stories about the university is how the medical program was started after the devastating 2010 earthquake that claimed 300,000+ Haitian lives. At the time, the program founders didn't have any idea that some of their *first students*—many of whom had been victims of the 2010 earthquake themselves—would eventually be among the *first responders* to the more recent 2021 earthquake, providing urgent medical care and compassion to their fellow Haitians. This story is one of thousands that speaks to the power of the organization's selfless service that continues to help people suffering in darkness.

Let Your Light Shine

I have a confession to make. Before I knew of Kristie and JeanJean's accomplishments, one of my motivations for traveling to Haiti had been selfish. (Another reason is that I had started reading one of my all-time favorite stories about the late Dr. Paul Farmer, who was a remarkable luminary and global leader in world health, in Tracy Kidder's book *Mountains Beyond Mountains*, which I highly recommend.) Unlike Dr. Farmer, I had hoped to visit Haiti to create a generous image of myself by posting pictures on social media of me helping poor people. Little did I know that I would be changed forever after visiting the Mompremiers during that adventurous first visit. The couple's selflessness opened my eyes to the miraculous things people can accomplish when they devote their lives to serving others.

We never know how our words and actions will impact people. One of the main reasons I've returned to Haiti almost every year since my first trip there is because Kristie and JeanJean invited me to join their story. The humble seeds of their selfless work have grown into a thriving garden of care that provides sustainable support for people in need. The Mompremiers are quintessential luminaries because they exemplify what it means to give back to the world, making them beacons of light for others to reflect.

Take Your Torch

You don't need to look beyond this morning's news headlines or corporate campuses to see how desperate the world is for more light.

Luminous work matters, whether you are serving communities with basic nutrition or serving your audiences with useful and inspiring stories. The most influential luminaries invite their audience members into their work to make their stories personally relevant.

You never know who your story will impact. JeanJean and Kristie's calling to start their nonprofit led to my calling to start LUV. Since then, my mission—in addition to illuminating tech leaders through story development—has been to give back and invite others into Haiti's story. Not only am I spotlighting the inspiring work being done by the Mompremiers, but I am also privileged to solicit support on their behalf. One hundred percent of the profits from the purchase of this book are going directly towards helping Haitians.

Thank you for joining and supporting their story. Now it's time for you to take your luminary lightsaber and "let your light shine."

ACKNOWLEDGMENTS

My story would not be possible without the selfless support of some special people over the course of my life. From early on my family has always been a rock of encouragement, especially my mom and dad (Terry and Kevin), my sister and brother (Sam and Ben), and my grandparents (Bernie and Hunzeek/Joan and Bo).

I also need to thank my high school speech and debate teacher (Mr. Matley) and college professors who planted seeds of interest in leadership and communications that are still bearing fruit today. Beyond educational influence, I'm forever indebted to the countless Yahoos who poured into my early career, especially the Events Team and Marissa Mayer for having taken a chance on me.

More recently, I owe deep gratitude to my incredibly talented and devoted LUV team (including my editor, Gary M. Krebs and this book's production team), as well as our inspiring clients who allow us to serve their people.

Lastly and most importantly, I started this book with a dedication to my wife and need to end the book with a special thank you to her. Words can't describe how grateful I am to our loving Light for stitching our stories together.

100 percent of the profits from this book will be donated to help families in Haiti (UCIhaiti.org). If you enjoyed the book, please leave a review on Amazon so we can support more technical professionals and help more Haitians.

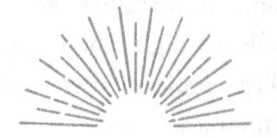

SUGGESTED READINGS

Aristotle. *Rhetoric.* University of Chicago, 2021.

Campbell, Joseph. *The Hero's Journey.* New World Library, 2014.

Covey, Steven. *The 7 Habits of Highly Successful People.* Simon & Schuster, 2013.

Cuddy, Ann. *Presence.* Little, Brown, 2018.

Duarte, Nancy. *Resonate.* John Wiley & Sons, 2010.

Gallo, Carmine. *Talk Like TED.* St. Martin's Press, 2014.

Goff, Bob. *Dream Big.* Thomas Nelson, 2020.

Goleman, Dan. *Emotional Intelligence: 10th Anniversary Edition.* Bantam, 2005.

Kidder, Tracy. *Mountains Beyond Mountains.* Random House, 2009.

Miller, Donald. *Building a StoryBrand.* HarperCollins, 2017.

Pink, Daniel. *Drive.* Riverhead, 2009.

Rosenberg, Marshall. *Nonviolent Communication, Third Edition.* Puddledancer Press, 2015.

Senge, Peter. *The Fifth Discipline.* Doubleday, 2016.

Shetterly, Margo Lee. *Hidden Figures.* William Morrow, 2016.

ABOUT THE AUTHOR

ER Harmon Photography

JACK GRIFFIN is founder and CEO of Light Up Ventures, an award-winning leadership development firm that coaches and trains Fortune 50 tech leaders to help optimize their performance. Jack has worked with 2,400+ speakers for a total of 10,000+ hours of development sessions with a range of professionals from highly technical individual contributors to top CEOs around the world. His passion for people has taken him to forty plus countries where LUV also supports underprivileged communities by donating twenty percent of their profits to philanthropic causes. Jack is also a proud Star Wars nerd and lives in the mountains of Northern California with his wife and three children.

TESTIMONIALS

"Jack helped me with intensive coaching before speaking at a large audience at an important conference. As you might expect if you know Jack, it went *very* well. Speaking at this conference has literally boosted my career to another level. I *will* be using Jack again the next time I have to speak, and you should too."

—George Talbot, Staff Software Engineer @ Google

"Jack coached me to deliver a recorded tech talk at a tech conference recently. I have delivered many tech talks before and was not sure if I really need not just one but two coaching sessions initially. But what a surprise! I've learned tremendously from Jack. Till today, I'm still applying Jack's tips and guidance on tech talks from drafting the presentation slides to the delivery methods."

—Qi Ke, VP of Engineering @ Microsoft

"Jack is an amazing coach with unusually broad experience. He had no problems relating to my particular dilemmas, and provided sage advice, along with a plan that has changed my ability to positively effect colleagues. I wholeheartedly recommend Jack."

—John Strassner, CTO @ Futurewei

"I worked with Jack to help me prepare for giving a technical talk at a conference in front of a large audience. He was very professional throughout the entire process—listening to our first draft of the presentation and offering helpful tips on structuring the talk to help keep the audience engaged, as well as advice on effective delivery, being comfortable on stage, and body language. This was my first talk in front of a large audience, and it went off smooth because of the preparation I had done with Jack; would highly recommend his services!"

—Peter Chng, Staff Software Engineer @ LinkedIn

"I recently presented and even though this was not my first conference talk, Jack's input has been very insightful and valuable. He made suggestions on how to better structure the presentation and the slide deck to align with the theme of the conference, how to make the back-and-forth transitions between co-speakers smoother and more natural, and many other improvements. I was initially dreading doing the dry runs, but it turned out to be a fairly enjoyable experience and certainly helped make the talk much better and more engaging. Thank you again, Jack!"

—Yuri Shkuro, Software Engineer @ Uber

"As an executive coach Jack is awesome. He guides you to become your best self professionally and personally. I had the pleasure of working with Jack as a client and would recommend his services."

—Carlene Zincke, Healthcare Consultant & Board Member

"Jack possesses a rare gift—to be able to articulate who you are now and what you need to do to achieve your aspiration. I could not articulate the block that I felt in my journey and it took Jack to help me chart my path. The amazing part is that it took him a few sessions to define me in a way that I could not. I am grateful for the lessons I have learnt."

—Anil Punyapu, Founder & CEO @ Uphealth

"I'm not a natural public speaker, but as I have progressed in my career, this has become a more and more important skill. I turned to Jack for some help both on structuring the content as well as honing my delivery skills.I was extremely happy with Jack's coaching. In a relatively short amount of time, he was able to teach me the basics of presentation structure and came up with a compelling framing for what I wanted to say. He was super creative, great to work with and very structured and goal oriented. He also walked me through the principles of how to give a presentation and through practice and coaching was able to get me to a confident place. My presentation was a great success and I got a lot of compliments for my delivery!

I was so satisfied that I asked Jack to give my leadership team a one-day training session with a short version of the training he gave me. This was also a great success with all of my team members saying that they felt more confident in their presentation skills. I find myself referring to the training when providing feedback on presentation and it's very handy to have a shared vocabulary that the team shares."

—Toby Negrin, Chief Product Officer @ Wikimedia

"Jack did a fantastic job coaching me for a talk at a tech conference. He gave very direct and impactful feedback and followed up with actionable and easy ways to address them. Jack made me realize that I was being a little robotic in my delivery and helped me present in a more conversational style. Overall, I really benefited quite a bit from working with Jack."

—Sazzala Reddy, CTO @ VMware

SOURCES

"Do. Or do not. There is no try."
https://www.starwars.com/news/the-starwars-com-10-best-yoda-quotes

"A dream written down with a date becomes a goal. A goal broken down into steps becomes a plan. A plan backed by action makes your dreams come true."
https://www.goodreads.com/author/quotes/905034.Greg_Reid#:~:text=Greg%20Reid%20Quotes&text=A%20dream%20written%20down%20with,makes%20your%20dreams%20come%20true

"One poll reported that only twenty percent of people set their own goals and, among that group, seventy percent fail…"
Vermeeren, Douglas, "Why People Fail to Achieve Their Goals," Reliable Plant.com, undated.
https://www.reliableplant.com/Read/8259/fail-achieve-goals

Introduction: 27 Seconds

"In 2012, on a summer day in the Silicon Valley of sunny California, former Google executive and employee #20, Marissa Mayer…"
https://swnsdigital.com/us/2018/12/it-takes-less-thank-30-seconds-to-make-a-first-impression/

"Research about first impressions has shown that that we have as little as ne-tenth of a second…"
https://clearly-speaking.com/first-impressions-matter-what-can-you-do-in-seven-seconds/

"Research shows that tech companies consider soft skills—particularly communication competence—in their performance reviews…"
   https://scholarworks.waldenu.edu/cgi/viewcontent.
   cgi?referer=&httpsredir=1&article=5180&context=dissertations
   https://www.nationalsoftskills.org/the-soft-skills-disconnect/
   https://www.linkedin.com/pulse/50-statistics-employee-communications-mvix-usa-/

"Whether you struggle with public speaking or don't stress about it, you likely have room…"
   https://scholarworks.waldenu.edu/cgi/viewcontent.cgi?referer=&httpsredir=1&article=5180&context=dissertations)
   https://www.nationalsoftskills.org/the-soft-skills-disconnect/
   https://www.linkedin.com/pulse/50-statistics-employee-communications-mvix-usa-/

"According to Merriam-Webster, the word luminary has two meanings…"
   https://scholarworks.waldenu.edu/cgi/viewcontent.cgi?referer=&httpsredir=1&article=5180&context=dissertations
   https://www.nationalsoftskills.org/the-soft-skills-disconnect/
   https://www.linkedin.com/pulse/50-statistics-employee-communications-mvix-usa-/

"Most technical efforts—involving both software and hardware—rely on light."
   https://www.crossrivertherapy.com/research/cell-phone-addiction-statistics

Chapter 1

"At 9:47 AM EST on February 20, 1962, the nation huddled around their television sets in anticipation…"
   https://www.nasa.gov/missions/project-mercury/mercury-atlas-6/

"In fact, it's estimated that eighty-three percent of our stress is related to work."
    https://www.zippia.com/advice/workplace-stress-statistics/

"The Project Management Institute reports that one third of all projects completely fail due to lack of communication…"
    https://www.linkedin.com/pulse/project-communication-risks-mitigation-yvan-c-/

"It makes the information more pertinent, relatable, and entertaining…"
    https://blog.stewartleadership.com/know-your-audience
    https://open.maricopa.edu/com225/chapter/need-to-find-audience-analysis-reading/

"…I want to close with a reference to the first wave of the 2020 COVID pandemic, when takeout food orders…"
    https://www.ncbi.nlm.nih.gov/pmc/articles/PMC9355939/.

Chapter 2

"The company struggled against rising competitive threats from tech giants such as Google…"
    https://www.nbcnews.com/tech/tech-news/it-s-not-just-marissa-yahoo-has-history-troubled-ceos-n696966

"Exposed to 4,000-10,000 advertisements per day."
    https://www.forbes.com/sites/forbesagencycouncil/2017/08/25/finding-brand-success-in-the-digital-world/?sh=3de5afca626e

"Spends two and a half hours per day on social media."
    https://www.statista.com/statistics/433871/daily-social-media-usage-worldwide/

"Checks email thirty-six times per hour."
    https://ppm.express/blog/checking-emails/.

"As if the above isn't enough, a recent study found that businesses lose $650B every year…"
https://www.thinkhdi.com/library/supportworld/2014/distraction-epidemic

"Eighteenth century philosopher Henry David Thoreau famously said, 'Our life is frittered away by detail…simplify, simplify.'"
https://www.brainyquote.com/topics/simplify-quotes

"As Nancy Duarte, author of the powerful book *Resonate*, recommends: 'The audience does not need to tune themselves to you…'"
https://www.duarte.com/what-does-it-mean-to-resonate/

"*Ethos*: This word translates to 'suffering' and 'experience.'"
https://www.linkedin.com/pulse/improving-business-communication-utilizing-aristotles-luke-kim/

"This is where Maslow's Hierarchy may be a useful tool to consider. The pyramid prioritizes basic human needs in order, from bottom to top: physiological…"
https://www.simplypsychology.org/maslow.html

Chapter 3

"Additionally, Elon Musk's company, SpaceX, has rocketed private space exploration into…"
https://www.spacex.com/launches/

"SpaceX has been remarkably efficient, lean, and economical with their efforts as well…"
https://www.valispace.com/why-spacex-and-tesla-move-faster-than-traditional-hardware-engineering-companies/

"Musk personally earns $6,887 per minute…"
https://news.abplive.com/technology/elon-musk-earning-per-week-400k-an-hour-second-networth-tesla-spacex-1664802

"To separate and address the latter, Musk and his teams regularly conduct spontaneous meetings known as *surges*…"
> https://www.cnbc.com/2023/09/11/elon-musk-moved-twitter-servers-himself-in-the-night-new-biography-details-his-maniacal-sense-of-urgency.html

"They're so modest that they openly share what occurred during one of the biggest tech outages in history in October 2021…"
> https://www.theguardian.com/technology/2021/oct/05/facebook-outage-what-went-wrong-and-why-did-it-take-so-long-to-fix

"According to James Cheo, Chief Investment Officer, at HSBC, people spend an average of 1.03 hours per day…"
> https://www.linkedin.com/posts/james-cheo-cfa-caia-frm-9677031_how-many-hours-do-most-people-spend-on-powerpoint-activity-7157614559422279680-X3TY/

Chapter 4

"One of the most influential books of all time is Stephen Covey's *The 7 Habits of Highly Successful People*."
> https://www.simonandschuster.com/books/The-7-Habits-of-Highly-Effective-People/Stephen-R-Covey/9781982137137

Chapter 5

"Personally, I don't find Webster's definition of the word story all that useful…"
> https://www.merriam-webster.com/dictionary/story#:~:text=%3A%20anecdote,narrative%20shorter%20than%20a%20novel

"One of my favorite quotes is from legendary filmmaker Alfred Hitchcock…"
> https://www.imdb.com/name/nm0000033/quotes/

"According to behavioral scientist and speaker Jennifer Aaker, 'Stories are remembered...'"
https://womensleadership.stanford.edu/node/796/harnessing-power-stories#:~:text=Stories%20are%20remembered%20up%20to%2022%20times%20more%20than%20facts%20alone.&text=When%20people%20think%20of%20advocating,more%20likely%20to%20be%20persuaded.

"Their servers can store 10,000-20,000 movies at the same time."
https://blog.uptrends.com/technology/binge-watching-how-netflix-content-is-stored-and-streamed/#:~:text=They%20use%2036%20drives%20that,10%2C000%20and%2020%2C000%20movies%20simultaneously.

"Even the company's vision speaks to storytelling: 'At Netflix, we aspire to entertain the world...'"
https://jobs.netflix.com/culture

Chapter 6

"This is the day I've been looking forward to for two and a half years..."
https://singjupost.com/wp-content/uploads/2014/07/Steve-Jobs-iPhone-2007-Presentation-Full-Transcript.pdf

"A basic principle of neuroscience is that our brains best recognize patterns in groups of three to help retain memory of them."
https://www.psychologytoday.com/us/blog/innovation-you/201507/the-wisdom-the-rule-three

"Instead, Kennedy cut to the chase with minimal words: 'Ask not what your country can do for you—ask what you can do for your country.'"
https://www.gilderlehrman.org/news/john-f-kennedy%E2%80%99s-inaugural-address-day-january-20-1961?gad_source=1&gclid=Cj0KCQjwvb-zBhCmARIsAAfUI2u3yjK-aXnrClXtGTGusyGRAvzOQJ5mK5HmcRlNk6fZXaWtOR-SoRm1gaAnVWEALw_wcB

Sources 203

"This quote from Nelson Mandela, the late President of South Africa, serves as a perfect example: 'I greet you all…'"
https://worldbicyclerelief.org/5-of-the-most-inspirational-nelson-mandela-quotes/?utm_term=nelson+mandela+quotes&utm_medium=ppc&utm_source=adwords&utm_campaign=World+Bicycle+Relief-The+Impact&hsa_cam=10575434340&hsa_ver=3&hsa_net=adwords&hsa_kw=nelson+mandela+quotes&hsa_tgt=kwd-214182596&hsa_ad=689598970994&hsa_grp=157985082629&hsa_mt=b&hsa_acc=9875632806&hsa_src=g&gad_source=1&gclid=CjwKCAjw-O6zBhASEiwAOHeGx-Q0cfok1gJr5KEG7K2gYYfDWHqsGqls4HVy0jL0Hd0meWsOU-QteNXBoCsXAQAvD_BwE

"This makes sense for two reasons: 1) ninety percent of information transmitted to the brain is visual…"
https://ifvp.org/content/why-our-brain-loves-pictures#:~:text=Images%20are%20superior%20to%20text,to%20the%20brain%20is%20visual.

"In 2012, James Chapman published an article in *Business Insider* that revealed the top ten most read books over the prior fifty years."
https://www.businessinsider.com/the-top-10-most-read-books-in-the-world-infographic-2012-12

"Neuroscientific studies have shown that we are hardwired to enjoy novelty because we release dopamine…"
https://www.inc.com/jeff-haden/neuroscience-says-your-brain-craves-new-for-dopamine-rush-but-research-shows-you-can-replace-that-sensation-much-more-productively.html#:~:text=A%20study%20published%20in%20Neuron,%2D%2D%20hard%20to%20resist.

"Carmine Gallo identified the following as Principle Five in his bestseller *The Presentation Secrets of Steve Jobs*: 'Create insanely different experiences.'"
https://www.carminegallo.com/steve-jobs-he-saw-genius-in-our-craziness/

Gurus such as Dale Carnegie famously taught, 'Tell the audience what you're going to say, say it; then tell them what you've said.'"
   https://quoteinvestigator.com/2017/08/15/tell-em/

"Convey your main points as media headlines as in this statement from Google CEO Sundar Pichai: 'Google teams have…'"
   https://www.facebook.com/watch/?v=982972409885201

"Neuroscience emphasizes the importance of primacy and recency for communication effectiveness."
   https://www.linkedin.com/pulse/rethinking-final-slide-why-neuroscience-warns-against-carmen-simon/

"There's an old Wayne Gretzky quote that I love. 'I skate to where the puck is going to be…'"
   https://singjupost.com/wp-content/uploads/2014/07/Steve-Jobs-iPhone-2007-Presentation-Full-Transcript.pdf

"For business presentations, I like to reference Donald Miller's book *Building a StoryBrand*."
   https://www.amazon.com/s?k=storybrand&i=stripbooks&crid=3S-GQ6LIQU3WV4&sprefix=storybrand%2Cstripbooks%2C81&ref=nb_sb_noss_1

"This is a breakthrough Internet communicator built right into [the] iPhone. The first rich HTML e-mail on a phone."
   https://singjupost.com/wp-content/uploads/2014/07/Steve-Jobs-iPhone-2007-Presentation-Full-Transcript.pdf

"The most amazing thing for me is that every single person who sees a movie, not necessarily one of my movies…"
   https://www.brainyquote.com/quotes/steven_spielberg_584115

Chapter 7

"In his bestselling book *Talk Like TED*, Carmine Gallo referenced an intriguing court case study as he…"
Gallo, Carmine. *Talk Like TED*. St. Martin's Press, 2014.

"Without getting into the technical weeds, my basic understanding of the intent of parameter tuning is to improve a system's ability to…"
https://www.alooba.com/skills/concepts/prompt-engineering/parameter-tuning/#:~:text=In%20the%20field%20of%20computer,software%20or%20system%20being%20used.

"If you know you struggle when it comes to confident body language, reflect on a study from Amy Cuddy's book, *Presence*…"
Cuddy, Ann. *Presence*. Little, Brown, 2018.

"In the meantime, I'll leave you with the following advice from social psycologist Amy Cuddy and her book *Presence*: 'Fake it until you become it.'"
Cuddy, Ann. *Presence*. Little, Brown, 2018.

Chapter 8

"In the meantime, to give you a head start, here is the link to his video…"
https://www.youtube.com/watch?v=Unzc731iCUY

"Churchill described his arduous preparation this way: 'If you want me to speak for two minutes…'"
https://www.azquotes.com/quote/858888

"This is especially important because audience members typically remember only ten to thirty percent of what they hear in presentations."
https://publicwords.com/2022/10/21/what-do-your-audiences-remember/

"According to an article from Michigan State University, it takes forty-seven facial muscles to frown and only thirteen to smile."
https://www.canr.msu.edu/news/what_does_a_smile_say

"When executed with the right restraint, timely hand gestures not only express your thoughts, but also convey your enthusiasm for the topic."
https://online.utpb.edu/about-us/articles/communication/how-much-of-communication-is-nonverbal/

"...researchers Joyce E. Bono and Remus Ilies discovered that subjects who rate high in upbeat charisma tend to invoke more favorable emotions from written and spoken communication than those on the low end."
https://www.researchgate.net/publication/222651742_Charisma_Positive_Emotions_and_Mood_Contagion

"A study orchestrated at the Olympic Training Center in Colorado Springs, CO found that one hundred percent of coaches and ninety-seven percent of athletes supported..."
https://members.believeperform.com/imagery-and-visualization-strength-and-conditioning-for-the-athletic-brain/#:~:text=One%20hundred%20percent%20of%20the,40%25%20used%20it%20for%20relaxation.

Chapter 9

'Tell the audience what you're going to say, say it; then tell them what you've said.'"
https://quoteinvestigator.com/2017/08/15/tell-em/

"The expression Emotional Intelligence (EQ) was originated by Peter Salovey and John D. Mayer in 1990."
https://www.emotionalintelligencecourse.com/history-of-eq/#:~:text=Peter%20Salovey%20and%20John%20D,guide%20one's%20thinking%20and%20action%E2%80%9D.

"Knowing one's emotions: self-awareness with recognition of feelings…"
https://www.thrivestreetadvisors.com/leadership-library/emotional-intelligence

"While there is some conflicting research on the matter, most studies have formed the conclusion that adults utter an average of 16,000 words per day."
https://wordsrated.com/how-many-words-does-the-average-person-say-a-day/

"On the flip side, the average person hears 20,000-30,000 words per day."
https://lightspeed-tek.com/you-need-to-hear-this-3-facts-you-didnt-know-about-listening/#:~:text=The%20average%20person%20hears%2020%2C000,U.S.%20suffer%20from%20hearing%20loss.

"To alleviate the intimidation, note another luminary of his time and is considered the founder of Taoism, Lao Tzu, who famously pronounced, 'A journey of a thousand miles…'"
https://www.brainyquote.com/quotes/lao_tzu_137141

"Jesus Christ, objectively one of the most influential communicators of all-time, encouraged 'Let your light shine before others…'"
https://www.biblegateway.com/passage/?search=Matthew%205%3A37&version=CEB

www.ingramcontent.com/pod-product-compliance
Lightning Source LLC
Chambersburg PA
CBHW070845310125
21141CB00044B/606